Tax Havens

What they are and what they can
do for the shrewd investor

Tax Havens

What they are and what they can do for the shrewd investor

ADAM STARCHILD

ARLINGTON HOUSE·PUBLISHERS
165 HUGUENOT STREET • NEW ROCHELLE, NEW YORK 10801

Copyright © 1979 by Adam Starchild

All rights reserved. No portion of this book may be reproduced without written permission from the publisher except by a reviewer who may quote brief passages in connection with a review.

Manufactured in the United States of America
P 10 9 8 7 6 5 4 3 2 1

Library of Congress Cataloging in Publication Data

Starchild, Adam.
　Tax havens.

　Bibliography: p.
　Includes index.
　1. Tax havens. 2. Tax planning—United States.
I. Title.
K4464.5.S7　　　343.05'2　　　79-19657
ISBN 0-87000-454-9

Contents

INTRODUCTION: OF MORALITY AND
   PATRIOTISM   9

PART ONE: TAX HAVENS IN THEORY AND PRACTICE

ONE / TAX REDUCTION: IS IT LEGAL?   13

TWO / WHAT ARE TAX HAVENS?   21

THREE / THE ROLE OF TAX HAVENS IN
   TAX PLANNING   33

FOUR / PUTTING TAX HAVENS TO WORK   39

FIVE / TAX HAVEN CORPORATIONS AND
   TRUSTS   65

SIX / SOME NOTES ABOUT TAXES   87

Part Two: The Tax Haven Guide

SEVEN / NO-TAX HAVENS: BALMY CLIMES FOR MONEY AND MAN   105

The Bahamas	108
Bermuda	115
The Cayman Islands	121
The New Hebrides	128

EIGHT / FOREIGN-SOURCE-INCOME HAVENS: PROFITS ABROAD, TAX FREE   135

Panama	137
Hong Kong	148
Liberia	154
Costa Rica	160

NINE / DOUBLE-TAXATION-AGREEMENT HAVENS: DOUBLE YOUR PLEASURE...   169

The Netherlands Antilles	172
The British Virgin Islands	178
Barbados	181

TEN / LIECHTENSTEIN: A BIT OF UTOPIA IN OLD EUROPE   183

ELEVEN / SWITZERLAND: LESS THAN MEETS THE EYE   217

EPILOGUE   223

APPENDIX / TAX HAVEN FACTS AND FIGURES   225

| Books to Read, Books to Avoid | 247 |
| Index | 249 |

Introduction:
Of Morality and Patriotism

This book will introduce you to a highly effective method of tax reduction. But who really wants to reduce his tax burden?

This question may seem stupidly naive. Who doesn't want to keep more of what's his? But this sort of answer, derived from the cynical "everyone is selfish," notion is not what we are looking for.

Tax reduction as outlined in this book requires considerable initiative, alertness, determination, and dedication. Not that it doesn't pay. Sad to say, the net gain from each hour dedicated to developing a tax reduction strategy is almost sure to be higher than the net gain from an hour of productive employment. Thanks to "progressive" taxation, this goes double for someone in a relatively high tax bracket.

There is also a psychological dimension to tax reduction that must not be neglected. Most people derive a "clean" feeling from making a living through their work, but feel that there is something "dirty" about "scheming" to reduce their taxes.

Heavy taxes, whether used to provide luxury for a ruling elite or to support welfare schemes, always have the effect of penalizing individual initiative and productivity, reducing investment capital and thus the resources required for economic growth, reducing the standard of living, and forcing individuals to hide things, both activities and incomes, from the government and from one another.

Heavy taxation is, therefore, a danger to the future of the United States. If more and more Americans would consciously and systematically act to reduce their individual tax burdens, they would not only improve their own lot, they would make a tremendous contribution to their country and the safety and freedom of the Western world. It is hoped that this book will make at least some small contribution to such a fight for individual liberty and national survival.

PART ONE:
Tax Havens in Theory and Practice

ONE

Tax Reduction: Is It Legal?

Tax lawyers and accountants usually like to stress the distinction between two seemingly similar methods of tax reduction: tax avoidance and tax evasion. It is important to understand this distinction, as well as to realize the limitations of its applicability to the ideas and information present in this book. At first glance, the distinction seems quite obvious. Tax avoidance is using whatever legal means are available to minimize a tax burden; tax evasion is the use of illegal means to the same end.

Using the services of an accountant, classifying certain verifiable expenses as "business expenses" with an acceptable, or seemingly acceptable, justification to reduce the taxable net income from one's business or profession is legal. Even if the IRS does not accept the validity of these deductions, and even, if worse comes to worse, all compromise attempts fail, the businessman doesn't have to fear being indicted for a criminal offense. The worst that can happen is that he will have to pay the tax he believed he didn't have to pay. This is tax avoidance.

On the other hand, willfully failing to report part of his income on his tax return or failing to comply with other reporting requirements is acting illegally. This is tax evasion.

Lawyers and accountants will explain, most sternly, that while they can help one to the best of their abilities to avoid taxes legally, by using all possible accounting tricks and legal loopholes, they will have nothing to do with tax evasion schemes. They cannot be accomplices to a crime; it could destroy them professionally, and anyway, they are law-abiding citizens. Thus, it would seem that the distinction between avoidance and evasion is very important.

However, once one looks into the matter, he will discover that the distinction is far from clearcut. Vagueness, ambiguity, and holes in the law make it unclear just what and how one is legally obliged to report. For instance, an investor is legally required to report any involvement he may have as a founder, shareholder, director, or officer of a new foreign-based corporation, or as a trustee, founder, or beneficiary of a foreign trust. (Both types of entities will be explained in detail below.) Once he makes such a report, the IRS takes care to demand from him an annual report of profits made by the foreign legal entity, even if these profits are not distributed to him and the other shareholders as income. On the basis of this report, and if the foreign corporation or trust satisfies certain extremely complex provisions of Subpart F of the U.S. Tax Code, the investor may be taxed on that part of the profits that corresponds to his proportion of ownership of or beneficial status in the foreign entity, even though nothing was paid to him in the United States. If he does not report involvement in the new company or trust, or doesn't report its business in a manner detailed enough to permit the IRS to infer whether he has Subpart F liabilities, or fails to pay taxes if he does have such liabilities, he is a criminal tax evader.

But let us take another example, a foreign corporation that an investor owns, lock, stock, and barrel. This foreign corporation did only one thing: In a third country, it created another corporation, which repeated the same exercise. Thus there came into being three foreign corporations: A, B, and C. The owner of A is legally obliged to report about A, and he reports truly that it has made no profit since its inception. He may even have to report that A created B. But since he personally owns no part of B, he does not have to report about B's activities. Company C, of course, is even less "report liable."

Let's say that C makes a substantial profit, which it reinvests. If C is liquidated and the proceeds are paid to the owner of A in the United States, the money becomes his taxable personal income. Not to report it is criminal tax evasion. But if C were quietly allowed to grow, and nothing were reported to the IRS . . . How could C be related to the owner of A, with C, B, and A in different countries, none of which exchange tax information with the U.S.?

Suppose further that registered shareholders of C, those whose names appear on documents that might reach the authorities, are just nominees, "proxy" shareholders who have private contracts with Company B giving it full control over their voting rights and full benefits from the dividends "their" shares earn each year. In this case, an investor could have nothing legally to do with C. If the IRS were to have the whole story, as told here, it might be able to prove a criminal conspiracy to evade income taxes.

But could the IRS dig out the whole story? Granted a complex enough structure of interrelated companies and proxy shareholders, one could easily defend in court a claim that he did not and could not know about all this. He did not get a cent out of it, as his bank accounts and books would show. He invested his money overseas, apparently unwisely, on the basis of some very arcane financial advice he only vaguely understood. There are many companies out there; his relationship to most of them is unclear. He did his legal duty as far as was possible by reporting his ownership of Company A. There is a limit to what an individual can be expected to report.

So what now? A lot depends on his lawyer. Still more important will be the judge's interpretation of the relevant tax code sections, complex, vague, ambiguous as they are, and his application of this interpretation to the complex facts of the case. What the judge does will depend on his legal erudition, familiarity with precedent, and political sympathies. (Is he a conservative with a secret dislike of the IRS? Is he a welfare statist? Is he a civil rights pioneer who believes one should pay income tax but that the IRS shouldn't violate individual privacy?) Even his daily mood can affect the outcome.

If a defendant loses the first round, he can appeal, introducing still more complexities.

The law, one's strategy, and a host of other factors may entail so much uncertainty that a harsh legal decision against the tax avoider could become unlikely. The defendant's lawyer may be convinced that his client is a genuine tax *avoider,* albeit a slightly clumsy one; the IRS lawyer may claim that he is an *evader;* the judge may reach an in-between verdict; the appeals courts may reverse the trial judge; and so on. Thus, the IRS may decide that the whole matter will cost more than what the government stands to gain and try to compromise out of court, or even drop the whole thing. On the other hand, it might try to make an example of the avoider/evader, going all out to force a new precedent and thus cow potential tax dodgers, and so on. In such a case as our example, anything can happen given our crazy tax laws, bureaucratic and political imperatives, and the imponderables of human nature. But even a clearcut, legal tax avoidance could be fought in court by the IRS and become, Wonderland-like, tax evasion.

Let us take an all too familiar example. A salesman claims as a business expense the cost of a dinner with a representative of another company in a very classy restaurant. The IRS, which has bugged the table, produces a recording of the dinner conversation to prove that the meeting was social rather than business; 95 percent of the talk was about the relative sexual merits of certain secretaries; only 5 percent was business. Did the salesman try to deceive the IRS and thereby evade taxes?

"No," he says, "it is well known in business circles that the guy I was dealing with does not sign any contract unless he is well drunk and has had an opportunity to brag about his sexual exploits. The sex talk was a necessary ingredient of business negotiations." But can he *prove* it? Can the IRS *disprove* it? Can the salesman sue the IRS for bugging the table—a violation of his privacy—and have the recording thrown out as evidence, voiding the case against him?

As you can see, there is no simple yes or no "criminal evasion" or "legal avoidance" answer in such situations. It all depends on the judge, the attorneys, the defendant's determination and resources, the IRS's determination and (vast) resources, the specific facts involved, the political context, and so on. Again, legal avoidance can all too easily be 1984ishly transformed into harshly penalized evasion. It can also work the other way round.

What must be borne in mind is that in practice there is a continuum between easy-to-discover tax avoidance, provable tax avoidance, and punishable tax avoidance. What one is faced with is a set of probabilities. His fate does not depend on hard and fast rules and facts, but on circumstantially determined chance. Some things he might do have very unclear legal status, and he may play for time, using complexity and good professional advice to guarantee himself almost complete safety.

While, for obvious reasons, it would be most unwise to tell a legal counsellor or accountant flat out that one plans tax evasion, this does not mean that it is not possible to discuss with them possibilities that are legally dubious. Tax *avoidance* terminology must be used, a language in which everything involved can be fully understood by all parties but that in no way smacks of criminal intent. The most important distinction to bear in mind is that between tax reduction methods that can lead one to court and prison and those that protect him from such consequences as well as protecting his money from the taxman.

The legal distinction between *avoidance* and *evasion* is the key here. If pushed, one may admit that he is involved in tax planning for tax avoidance purposes—strictly within the letter of the law—and that he abhors tax evasion as much as the next guy. There is no simple legal classification applicable to most approaches. Our dinner example illustrates this point. Indeed, in this typical case, would you be able to decide *for certain* that the classification of the dinner as business-related is or is not legally correct? Presumably, the salesman wouldn't have held the dinner for other purposes. Presumably, he would have eaten something anyway. Presumably, he would not have invited his wife to a true business meeting. Presumably, he did so because the other guy invited his wife at the salesman's expense, indicating he does not do business with anyone who eats out without his frau. (We are changing the story to overillustrate the point.) Who could tell? Even the salesman cannot be entirely sure about it.

Put simply, in tax matters, one should steer clear of stupid actions that will surely result in indictment and conviction for tax evasion. If a person has "black" money in a foreign bank account in his own name and this is proved in court, he's had it—and deserves it.

As you read the following chapters, you should keep in mind that this is *not* a handbook, that I am *not* counselling any course of action. *Tax Havens* is a source book, designed to provide information on tax havens, their nature, and their possible uses in tax planning. What the reader does with this information is strictly up to him.

Two

What Are Tax Havens?

No investor can rely on the tax haven approach as an element of his tax-minimization strategy unless he has a full understanding of what tax havens are. It is also necessary to become thoroughly familiar with the ins and outs of the several kinds of tax havens available.

Simply stated, a tax haven is any country whose laws, regulations, traditions, and, in some cases, treaty arrangements make it possible for one to reduce his overall tax burden. This general definition, however, covers many types of tax havens, and it is important to understand their differences.

No-Tax Havens. These are countries that have no income, capital gains, or wealth (capital) taxes, and in which it is possible to incorporate and/or form a trust. The governments of these countries do earn some revenue from corporations; "no-tax" means that what is paid is independent of income derived through a company. These states may impose stamp duties on documents of incorporation, a small charge on the value of corporate shares, annual registration fees, etc.

In some of these no-tax havens, a corporation is presented with the sharp alternative between being allowed to deal locally and being exposed to the prospect of paying income taxes in some unspecified future in which they may or will be imposed, and being able to deal locally and having a long-term (however specified) guarantee against future taxation (being an "exempt" company). The second kind of situation may seem to be just the thing if one has no real business interest in the haven itself. But one of the relevant considerations for the application of certain important IRS code provisions is whether or not a company does any local business in its domicile country; that is, does the company have a real "business justification," or is it just a tax dodge? (These provisions of the tax laws will be discussed in detail in a later chapter.) If because of its officially exempt status in a tax haven a company cannot do any local business, its American owner may find himself paying unwanted U.S. taxes.

No-Tax-on-Foreign-Income Havens. These countries do impose income taxes, both on individuals and corporations, but only on *locally derived* income. They exempt from tax any income earned from foreign sources that involve no local business activities apart from simple "housekeeping" matters. For example, in such a haven there is no tax on income derived from export of local manufactured goods.

The no-tax-on-foreign-income havens break down

into two groups. There are those that allow a corporation to do business both internally and externally, taxing only the income coming from internal sources, and those that require a company to decide at the time of incorporation whether it will be one allowed to do local business, with the consequent tax liabilities, or one permitted to do only foreign business and thus be exempt from taxation. Again, it may seem that the latter approach is better—but the matter of "business justification" may be an important consideration.

Low-Tax Havens. These are countries that impose some taxes on all corporate income, wherever earned. However, most have double-taxation agreements with the United States that may reduce the withholding tax imposed on income derived from the U.S. by local corporations.

Special Tax Havens. These are countries that impose all or most of the usual taxes, but either allow special concessions to special types of companies or allow very special types of corporate organization, such as the very flexible corporate arrangements offered by Liechtenstein.

Immigration Countries. In the last century, the United States was the major immigration country of the world. Today, its tax policies may motivate some to go where they can pay fewer and lower taxes. In principle, of course, any no-tax haven could be such an immigrant paradise. But many of these countries do not want immigrants because they are overcrowded, because they have serious unemployment problems, or because of a whole host of other reasons. Also, most of these countries are underdeveloped, and even though one's income would be untaxed, it would likely be lower than what he could earn in the U.S.—even after taxes.

The true immigration havens are those countries where Americans are officially welcome and where one could retire and live on income from investments, pension plans, etc., derived from U.S. sources, but free of the U.S. tax burden. This could mean having to give up one's American passport, but some of these countries offer a new passport immediately.

Even if one has already made up his mind about the structure of his tax-minimizing program, combining, say, a no-tax haven, a low-tax haven, and ultimate immigration, he still must know much more about each country under consideration before taking the plunge. It is not enough to know that X is a "tax haven"; it is not enough to know that one's lawyer likes its beaches. The tax minimizer must have both general knowledge about country X and specific knowledge about current political and social developments there: he certainly does not want to wake up one morning to a call advising that all his corporate assets have been confiscated by the new military government of X, or that no funds can be sent out of the country, or that the new corporate profits tax is 85 percent. Things like this rarely happen. But they do happen. The only insurance against them is comprehensive advance knowledge on the country or countries one plans to get involved in and keeping the information current. In particular, the following must be known:

Costs. A tax haven country usually derives substantial revenue from its "tax haven industry." This means there are charges that must be borne by any company chartered there: government fees (stamp duties, some form of stock-value charge) and non-government costs (legal fees, trust company charges, etc.).

In view of the fact that it may be necessary to have more than one tax haven company in more than one country to take care of things, these costs may weigh heavily in deliberations. Original incorporation costs are only the beginning. Usually, some sort of "legal presence" in the country of incorporation is required: an office with a sign bearing the company name, a local director or legal representative, etc. These services are available, but they cost, and in some places they cost more than in others. When deciding on tax-saving methods, the costs must be run against the tax savings. With relatively small amounts of investment funds, the tax haven approach may never be worthwhile. However, in view of the fact that the costs are essentially fixed, bearing no relation to the size of income involved, the larger the gross from investment, the less important are the expenses of using tax havens.

Flexibility of Corporate Structure. Some tax havens may require that stockholders' meetings be annual and local. This may require an annual visit to the haven. If keeping things "low-profile" is important, this could be a serious disadvantage. It also costs money and is a nuisance. There may be a requirement for "minimum paid-in capital" at the time of incorporation. This may, in some places, be got around through a local ad hoc loan from a local bank. In other places it may not, and the loan may be expensive. Another problem may be the required number of local corporate directors, or the need for more than one local shareholder, etc. Local firms are available to "ease" such official requirements on corporate structure by providing proxies, and such, but this involves extra expense, expense that cannot be written off as a deduction against U.S. taxes.

Exchange Controls and Monetary Freedom.
Since using a tax haven corporation usually involves a flow of funds in and out of the haven country, the issue of the freedom to conduct such exchanges is crucial. To what extent is one free to take money out of the country? If there are severe restrictions, the place is no haven. Rhodesia has a flat income tax of 5 percent. It could be a tax haven, if not for the fact that it is illegal take money out of the country. Similarly, are there any restrictions on converting U.S. dollars into local currency and vice versa? Are special permissions required for each exchange? General permission with reports on each exchange? General permission with no official control but with all exchanges restricted to officially approved agencies at fixed official ratios? Or is there a free money market? Can one deal as he pleases outside the country in U.S. dollars, keep an account in them locally, but be completely debarred from converting them to local currency? Can local currency generated by local business be converted to U.S. dollars?

Detailed answers to these questions are very important.

Accessibility. Quick communication may be crucial to efficient utilization of a tax haven. Suppose it is necessary to instruct a haven company to make a quick stock purchase, but the haven lies in the other hemisphere, where it is after midnight. Suppose there is only one telephone in the building of the company agent, shared with seventy-five other offices, and it is usually out of order. Suppose cables are delivered only once a week, airmail is nonexistent, and surface mail takes eight months for a roundtrip. This is an extreme example, but in some cases it is not too far off the mark. These things must always be considered: Is there speedy, reliable telephone, telegraph, telex, and airmail communication? Is the place accessible by air, directly or indirectly? By sea? By land? If one can get there without too much difficulty, will the government let him in?

Professional Services. Tax haven activities involve many related professionals: lawyers, bankers, trust managers, accountants. Some tax havens may be too small or underdeveloped to have acceptable services. If there is but one local lawyer who is at the same time the country's only accountant and a barber in his free time (or perhaps the other way around), forget it.

Apart from these obvious considerations, there are some subtler ones. Are all the local banks representatives of major American banks? It might be deceptively convenient to arrange everything through the Chase Manhattan Bank, relying on its local branch in the tax haven to handle money transfers and so on. Undeniably, Chase Manhattan is a good, reliable bank. Unfortunately, records of such arrangements are all too accessible to prying eyes.

With completely independent foreign banks, one has to be careful too. Some havens have very flimsy banking regulations. This may be good in general, but there's always the danger of a fly-by-night outfit. This is true of any professional service overseas. One should not go overboard with suspicion, but things must be carefully checked out in advance.

Language and Tradition. Tax haven business requires cross-cultural communication. This can be disrupted by language barriers and matters of legal tradition and practice. In general, countries that share the Anglo-Saxon common law tradition are the best tax haven bets. There is usually the added advantage of English being an official language.

Possibilities for Local Business Activities. Some tax havens may offer you positive business reasons for local investment quite apart from any tax considerations. Such reasons include subsidies and other special treatment, low labor costs, etc. Other havens may strictly forbid any "exempt" company from local business dealings.

Political and Social Stability. This is, needless to say, the most important consideration of all. It determines and affects all the rest. A country that is involved in a civil war, or that regularly changes governments "by bullet," or that has a strong socialist political faction is hardly to be trusted to keep investment assets secure. A political upheaval, or even a change in legislation introducing taxes or other restrictions on corporations or trusts, may take away everything. What are the indications of stability and unstability? Clearly, there are no foolproof signs, but there are things that do help formation of an intelligent judgment.

History. A country that has had very moderate political, economic, racial, and social change over the years, where political and social violence are not common, can be deemed to possess a tradition of conservative peacefulness. A tradition is an almost tangible social force. It moulds a people's way of thinking and acting, and it is a good predictor of stability.

There are, of course, more specifically segmented predictors of stability. A country that has never had any form of income taxation can be counted on to have a population that would be less than sanguine about the imposition of such taxation. This may apply even if there is some other form of political instability, say, regular military coups. Such coups could be totally irrelevant to any economic development, because economic legislation and public service may be unaffected by which general currently happens to occupy the presidential palace.

Population. A racially diverse population *may* mean racial tensions that could bring about some form of social or political upheaval. In some places, though, there is completely peaceful coexistence between European and non-European citizens.

Political-Economic Situation. There is a wide range of variables here. If a country has a one-house, popularly elected legislature and a very active socialist government, it will not remain a tax haven for long. If it has a government divided, say, between a governor general (representing the crowned head of the "mother country") and a locally elected two-house legislature, and there is little local political dissension, radically adverse legislation is not especially likely.

General poverty *may* be indicative of a potential for revolution, while stable prosperity is more promising. Trade union activity of any consequence may be indicative of a potential for socialism in the future. A government with strong motivations for "progress" may be a mixed blessing. Such a regime may encourage overseas investors and at the same time increase welfare budgets and thereby create a future need for heavy taxes. Universities with politically active leftist student bodies are bad signs.

Prospects for Foreign Invasion and War. These are slighter for an isolated island country than a continental country, but in the latter case, things to consider are: Which continent? Which neighbors? It is quite unlikely for Liechtenstein to be invaded by Germany, Italy, or France. But what are the prospects for Rhodesia (assuming for illustration that it is a tax haven)?

In my survey of tax havens, to be presented in part two, "The Tax Haven Guide," I have screened out those countries that superficially could be classified as tax havens. I will not elaborate on the Hungarian "competition" to Swiss numbered bank accounts. I will also pass in relative silence over Israel's claim to be a tax haven for certain foreign investors. Whatever might be the attractions of its specific tax laws pertaining to such investors, a country that has gone through five wars in thirty years, that has an inflation rate of more than 100 percent and heavy exchange controls, where devaluation happens monthly, trade unions are rampant, and racial tensions are explosive, is not a reliable haven of any sort.

I have selected only countries that possess some credible stability and that can really compete on the tax haven market. Each has its own specific advantages and disadvantages. It is up to the individual investor to decide which are best suited to his needs and circumstances.

THREE

The Role of Tax Havens in Tax Planning

This is not an exhaustive handbook of tax avoidance methods. Rather, it is designed to bring to the reader's attention a specific method of tax avoidance that can be used in combination with other, more conventional methods, not as an alternative to them.

To understand the precise role of tax havens, it is important to distinguish two basic sorts of income: (1) return on labor and (2) return on capital. The first kind of return is what one gets from his *work:* salary, wages, fees for professional services, and the like. The second kind of return relates, basically, to the return from *investments:* dividends on shares of stock; interest on bank deposits, loans, and bonds; rental income; royalties on patents.

It is the second kind of income, income from an investment portfolio, that tax havens are useful for. If one does nothing about it, this income is treated for tax purposes in essentially the same fashion as salary and wages. If the resulting tax bracket is reasonably high, investment returns are "punished" much more severely than work-originated income since it is difficult to apply to it tax-saving measures related to concessions, allowable deductions, etc.

There are ways other than the use of tax havens to defend this investment income against heavy taxes. All of them involve a common principle: reduction of the applicable tax bracket through legal alienation of income. For example, if an executive's salary is $25,000 a year and his gross return on investments is $5,000, the extra $5,000 is taxed, if considered a part of his income, at the rates applicable to income in the $25,000 to $30,000 range. If, however, he gives his wife the stock, and she has no further income, she is taxed according to the much lower rates that apply to an annual income of $5,000 (assuming they file separately). There may be an initial tax penalty in the form of a gift tax on the stock transfer. It is a matter of calculation to find out the most economical way of making such a change of ownership. On the other hand, the transfer could save estate taxes and probate expenses when the husband dies. The precise calculation is complex and may involve such hard-to-measure considerations as the relative likelihood of a divorce somewhere down the road.

But what we are interested in here is the principle of *alienation:* transferring to some different legal person income that would have otherwise gone to the alienator, thereby making use of the fact that the other legal person is subject to lower tax rates.

Why did I use the term *legal person?* One's wife is both a legal and a real person, of course. She is a legal person, with personal assets and responsibilities, because she is a human being. But the same principle is illustrated by another method of alienating income: incorporation.

A corporation is as much a legal person as a human being. It has separate assets, separate liabilities, separate income, and separate tax burdens. In the United States, corporations pay a flat tax rate (46 percent) on their net incomes. Thus, if a businessman (1) incorporates his business; (2) hires himself as a corporate employee with a modest salary; (3) deducts all conceivable business expenses—including, of course, his salary and those he may pay to members of his family—(4) pays corporate income tax on the company's net profit at a flat rate that should be less than he would have had to pay had the income been his personally; (5) takes the net profit after tax and pays himself out of it the minimally allowable dividend (there are, usually, some legal requirements that some minimum percentage of the net profit of a corporation after taxes has to be distributed as dividends); (6) makes his wife, daughter, son *et al.* stockholders (taking into account the gift tax) and pays them dividends as well, thus taking advantage of their lower tax brackets; and (7) reinvests the rest of the profits in the growth of the company, he should be considerably better off in the tax department.

Needless to say, this is not a sufficiently detailed "how-to" plan, but it illustrates the point. Taxes are lower on the combined income derived from salary (or salaries) and dividends than the incorporator would have paid if the net profit all around were his personal income. Also, by reinvesting corporate profits that have never been part of personal income, he increases the value of his company and, thus, the value of his holdings in it. Later on, if he sells the stock, the profit from the sale is a capital gain. The tax rates on capital gains are usually much lower than regular income tax rates on comparable income. Thus, the principle used here is *alienation of income for reduction of applicable tax rates through lowering of applicable tax brackets.*

The kind of arrangements outlined above are probably well known to the reader from his own experience. He may very likely have used similar methods himself. There are, as yet, no tax havens involved. Observe, however, that two specific features of the tax system *are* involved, each giving rise to a distinct tax-minimizing principle: (1) Taxes are imposed on *net* income. This gives rise to the principle of *maximizing* deductible expenses and thus *minimizing* recorded, taxable net income. (2) Taxes are levied "progressively," with increasing rates on higher income brackets. This gives rise to the principle of alienating income to legal entities whose applicable brackets are lower than those of the alienator. These entities may be real people with little or no other income, or corporations, whose applicable tax rates may be lower than the incorporator's.

These two principles are, essentially, the same as those involved in tax planning when tax havens are used. If our income tax system imposed taxes on *gross* income at a flat rate, these two principles would not apply, and taxes could not be minimized. If, indeed, the tax rate were reasonably low, there would be little motivation for such action. However, even with a uniform rate on all gross incomes, these two principles could still help to reduce taxes through tax havens in a fashion not available here at home. This is because tax havens introduce a third principle, that of the free market.

Different countries have different tax policies and laws, and one can, in principle, alienate part of his investment income to a business entity in another country. Thus, to give a very simplistic example—one that does not take into account all the complications that we will have to consider later in our discussion—if an investor incorporates in, say, Bermuda, which is a no-tax country, and vests his entire portfolio there, instead of paying, say, U.S. taxes of 48 percent of his investment income, he would pay nobody anything. He would thus be able to reinvest the *entire* yearly yield on his portfolio in more stock.

It is easy to see that over twenty years there is a big difference between reinvesting gross dividends and after-tax dividends. Even if our hypothetical investor liquidates his company after forty years, "repatriates" the profits to the U.S., and pays taxes on them as a one-year income (which would put him in a very high bracket!), the multiplier effect of reinvesting "whole dollars" would still not be entirely wiped out.

Alternatively, when he decides to retire, he could immigrate to a friendly country that likes Americans so much that it does not tax their incomes from abroad (there is such a place!) and start receiving dividends there from his no-tax-haven company, as well as any superannuations, pension, social security, etc., due from the United States. Another possibility for him would be to leave his stock in a foreign trust (which we will discuss in detail below) with his family members as beneficiaries, thereby avoiding inheritance taxes.

Obviously, the foregoing case is a huge oversimplification. (We will deal with the qualifications and complexities later, as well as the extra costs they incur.) If things *were* so simple, U.S. tax revenues would have dried up years ago. Nonetheless, many have found the effort and study required to learn how to use the tax haven road to riches well worth it indeed.

FOUR

Putting Tax Havens to Work

Tax havens offer a possibility for tax savings that cannot be matched by any other approach to tax avoidance. However, the precise use of tax havens depends very much on one's particular circumstances, objects, and concerns.

The use of tax haven corporations requires expenditures for both incorporation and corporate maintenance. Very roughly, $1,000 a year (including the year of incorporation) per company is what can be expected. An investor must have investment capital on the order of $10,000 to consider using a tax haven. And since most "foolproof" tax haven plans require at least a double-tier combination to take full advantage of haven benefits, at least two corporations are necessary, doubling the sum to be put in. Only when investible savings total at least $20,000 can one get lucratively involved in tax havens on a full-scale basis. Five years of work and saving may bring a person into this investment class, but even if he is not yet there, it is worth starting today to plan for the future.

Another point that must be considered is what is to be done with the proceeds from tax haven investments. Will it pay for luxurious pleasure trips? Will it underwrite retirement in comfort and security? Or will it be left to loved ones? In the latter case, a tax haven trust may allow one to transfer his estate to his family with all the benefits of money growth in a haven and without the burden of inheritance taxes.

These points indicate that whether and how one should get involved in tax havens depends upon his investment capital and his personal plans concerning the earnings from it. To come to a sound conclusion, one must compute, with the aid of an accountant and a tax advisor, the tax liabilities and expenses he would have to meet for the forthcoming years, based on the best available estimates, and then run these figures against estimated tax savings and extra costs incurred by the use of tax havens. And he must make up his mind *now,* not later. A later change of mind could cost a pretty penny.

Another consideration is the effect that tax havens have on the nature of investments. As we will see shortly, a tax haven corporation that has U.S. investments—whether in securities or in real estate—is open to an IRS challenge under Subpart F of the tax code on the grounds that it is a "controlled holding company." Investments in the United States have the additional liability of being subjected to a 30 percent U.S. withholding tax on the gross income generated in the U.S. and remitted abroad. This withholding tax can be reduced by proper utilization of tax havens that have double-taxation agreements with the United States. The Subpart F issue is more serious because once one is hit with it, his tax haven setup loses all viability. Still, one may prefer U.S. investments for business reasons.

Clearly, an investor must change his perspective concerning his investments when considering the use of havens. To firmly delineate the nature of this change, let us make some distinctions between investment orientations.

"Pure Business." This is the attitude the IRS wants an investor-businessman to have. It means that he is expected to plan his investment (and life) with the central objective of making a maximum gross profit—and to pay the maximum taxes attached to such success. A more reasonable man will utilize the services of an accountant to minimize the tax penalty, but tax considerations are not supposed to affect any business decision. They may affect accounting and bookkeeping, directed at keeping a very good record of all deductible expenses, but not how or where one does business. This is the attitude one may have to feign if his tax haven corporation comes under unsympathetic scrutiny. Thus it pays to have a sound, "pure business" reason for setting up shop in a far-off land.

Pure Tax Planning. This may be the attitude of somebody who keeps his income so low as to be untaxable or who immigrates to a no-tax country. Here the motivation is the exact reverse of "pure business": This person does not want maximum profit; he wants minimum taxes. Some tax rebels are ideologically motivated to do just that. They forget about how much money they have in their pockets and concentrate on how they can fend off the IRS pickpockets. This may also be the attitude of a tax martyr who files his annual return with a refusal to fill it in on Fifth Amendment grounds. If this is the reader's attitude, good luck. If not, read on.

Net-Profit Planning. This attitude is not based on the desire to make the U.S. Treasury richer, nor on the desire to make it poorer. It is based on the objective of maximizing the money left over after the taxman extracts Uncle Sam's cut. In other words, gross profits concern the net-profit planner only insofar as he needs them, for accounting purposes, to calculate tax rates and net profits. And the IRS concerns him only as a kind of undesired creditor whose share in the profits is to be minimized. His net profits are not monies that his accountant classifies as such; they are monies he can use to achieve his own life purposes, to do with as he pleases. Whether they are on the books as "business expenses" or "salary" or "rent on the company car," or what have you, is a matter that concerns the net-profit planner only to the extent that there is always the possibility that the IRS might decide that what he has classified as business expenses were actually personal expenses.

This approach underlies everything offered in this book. The principles and ideas herein are for people who want to increase their purchasing power, the money they can use as they wish. The legal or accounting label for the money—whether one "owns" it or merely controls it—matters little. Similarly, the view on capital taken here is that only a fool would maximize the amount of capital he *owns,* in the sense of having direct, personal legal title to it. What should be of primary interest is the capital one can control, dispense with as he sees fit, whatever or whoever has formal title to it.

Contemporary attitudes and politics have transformed ownership and profits into "social sins" and tax liabilities. Therefore, the tax minimizer should seek control and usable assets available in such forms that avoid these strictures. This line of thinking is important in trying to assess whether or not to use the simplest form of tax haven: the offshore fund.

Offshore Funds. At first sight, an offshore fund is the ideal means of utilizing the advantages of tax havens without falling prey to their disadvantages. An offshore fund is an internationally financed corporation based in a tax haven. It operates by selling stock to the public, and it invests the monies for the stockholders in a manner that, ideally, gets maximum possible "gearing," doubling the invested funds as quickly as possible. The profits are reinvested in turn, and since the offshore fund is based in a haven, it pays no taxes on its profits and can reinvest whole dollars.

Such a setup gives these apparent advantages: (1) An investor can enjoy the benefits of a haven without incurring the costs of creating his own company. (2) He can "forget" about the troubles of deciding how best to invest his money. By buying a share of an offshore fund, he is buying the services of professional investment managers who will optimally invest his money for him. (3) He can usually forget about Subpart F. Since offshore funds are international, and thus have stockholders in virtually every industrialized country, they usually do not "qualify" as being American controlled. Thus, the investor may not have to worry that any part of his fund's undistributed profits will be taxed to him. (4) Offshore funds do not usually pay dividends because they reinvest all profits. This means that personal income tax liability is not increased. (5) The investor's personal means of claiming his share of the fund's profits when he wants to is to sell his shares in the fund. If the fund does well, its stock will go up, and the investor will have a gross capital gain. This is taxable, but usually at a rate much lower than regular income. (There are ways of eliminating or reducing capital gains taxes, but even if these are ignored, the investor has still saved taxes by allowing them to be deferred over the years and by using the leverage of reinvestment of whole dollars through the fund.) (6) Tax haven offshore funds are free of U.S. government regulations imposed on American investment companies. Domestic companies are required to invest in ways sufficiently "conservative" that the "small investor's" money will not be risked on "chancy" ventures. But an offshore fund can take advantage of a "risky investment" to give the maximum return in a short time. A competent offshore fund manager should be attentive to the security of money entrusted to him because he depends on his reputation to stay in business. Thus, one can expect considerable security coupled with a very quick rate of increase in the value of his investment. The prospects for a high and speedy rate of return are enhanced by the fact that most tax havens are not only nontax countries but highly free enterprise countries, where substantial decisions of corporate executives are not hampered by regulations and red tape.

Thus, offshore funds should, in principle, couple both gross-profit benefits, coming from cleverly calculated "speculative" investment utilizing the whole range of possibilities of the world economy, and net-profit benefits, avoiding the trouble and expense of finding an accountant and a lawyer to help with incorporation, the fees associated with incorporation, the burden of managing one's own investment, etc. Further, such funds do not require the relatively large amounts of capital needed to take advantage of other approaches.

All in all, offshore funds seem to offer the full benefits of tax havens at a bargain price—the ideal get-rich-quick-with-small-cost-no-worries scheme. However, while all of these advantages are real, they all hinge on one crucial factor: the honesty and competence of the individuals who run the offshore fund. Government regulations on investment companies do restrict the profitability and capital growth of such companies, but they also guarantee some sort of minimal security to the investor. They serve to screen out, however inefficiently, the straight-out crooks and the impractical dreamers who are frequently taken in by the crooks. In other words, whenever one transfers management of his own investment portfolio to an investment manager, either directly or by buying shares in an investment fund, he must be on the lookout for crooks, fools, and the lethal combination of the two. Any get-rich-quick scheme, whether or not initially viable and valid, attracts the scam artists and the dreamers, and together they generate a fantasy industry that all too quickly turns into a nightmare for the unwary investor.

Offshore funds are completely unregulated. One's only security is his own verification of the personal integrity and professional competence of the people running the fund he buys into. There are no shortcuts to verifying such information. Even what seems to be on paper, even "verified" paper, a very large and promising fund can be large because many fools, manipulated by very clever crooks, goaded by other fools, or both, have bought lots of stock. What looks good in a bright, shiny, beautifully produced prospectus may turn out to be an elaborate fraud not worth the paper on which the slick presentation is printed. If one cannot verify beyond a reasonable doubt the ethical and professional credentials of the people running the show, he should not put his money into it. Period.

To emphasize this point from another angle, one may be motivated by ideological considerations. There are many libertarians and conservatives who consider antitax measures to be of primary ideological significance, over and above the money remaining in their pockets. Some clever manipulators, aware that an ideologically motivated person may easily and blindly trust someone who behaves and talks as if he were similarly motivated, will offer "fantastic investment possibilities" laced with the appropriate ideological buzz words. The ideologically motivated "investor" would feel safe with, say, "a fellow libertarian." He could not be deceitful or stupid. He would certainly protect one's investment and handle it with great care and wisdom. Anyone who approaches his investment decisions this way should not be surprised to find himself on the short end of the stick—if indeed there is a stick. There's a con artist out there for every sucker. Beware.

Before investing in an offshore fund, an investor *must* study the track records of the fund and the people running it. How many years has the fund existed? How has its stock behaved? What kind of profits has it made? What investments has it made, and how many of them were considered risky and then proved to be successful? How many were risky and wound up disasters? How many were prudent? As for the fund managers, what were they doing before they set up or took over the fund? How successful were they? What makes them personally reliable? What supports their claims that their investment judgment is sound?

All of these considerations may squelch any interest the reader may have had in offshore funds. This is not our intention. Rather, the purpose of raising these considerations is to make the reader aware of certain very important facts: (1) Whenever considering buying stock in *any* company—offshore fund, local investment company, or what have you—one should judge only by computing the probable net increase in net purchasing power resulting from the investment. Business advantages and profits and tax benefits should be computed together, not separately. An offshore fund should be evaluated as any other company, but in view of its special dependence on the personal qualities of those running it, a little bit more carefully. (2) It is a fallacy to think in general-category terms about offshore funds. While they share some general characteristics, they vary enormously, as do the persons running them. Specific companies and individuals must be evaluated, not the general concept.

It is in light of these considerations that we should recall the history of offshore funds. They mushroomed in the early 1960s. The Subpart F regulations, introduced in 1964, enhanced their attraction, for the international stock ownership of most funds clearly exempted them from any application of Subpart F. Some funds, however, most notoriously IOS and Gramco, tried to outdo their competitors by making very high-risk investments; had they been lucky, the high risk would have been translated into high profits, and this would have pushed up the value of their stock and allowed them to expand by issuing new shares. (Most offshore funds are incorporated with the flexibility of issuing more shares and increasing their authorized capital and, alternatively, buying back shares and cancelling them to reduce their authorized capital.) Lady Luck, however, is fickle, and these two companies, among others, crashed rapidly. No detectable fraud was involved in the IOS and Gramco cases, but their bad management, so hopeful for big growth as to neglect the perils, managed to reduce the reputation of tax havens in general, and offshore funds in particular.

Nonetheless, offshore funds still remain viable investment opportunities. Most of them offer privacy because they are registered in countries where even the shareholder register is not open to any official inspection. Combined with their investment potential, unhampered by regulation, and the fact that the only possible taxes are withholding taxes in the countries in which their investments are located, they offer, in principle, a good hunting ground. But one must hunt very carefully, observing track records, individual and corporate, and disregarding vague though beautiful promises and propaganda.

Together with these considerations, the following points on personal income taxation as it relates to the money earned on offshore investments should be considered. In general, offshore funds are international in ownership. But it must be certain that the share composition of the proposed fund does not give the appearance of "American control." One would be on the safe side if not more than 50 percent of the stock is held by Americans. Even if the share composition is all right, if more than 60 percent of the fund's gross "passive" income (earnings derived from investments rather than production or trade) comes from the United States, the IRS may consider it to be a "controlled personal holding company" and penalize the American owners with a 70 percent tax on the undistributed profits of the company to the extent of their ownership. For example, if one owns one percent of the stock issued by such a fund that makes an undistributed profit of $1 million, one percent of that will be considered to be his income. He will be required to pay a tax on money he has never seen!

Thus, both the share composition of an offshore fund and its sources of passive income are things to be checked out before investing. This may seem like a lot of trouble, but, remember, there is no way to profitably take advantage of good opportunities without very careful evaluation of a very large body of facts. If one does his homework, is satisfied about Subpart F considerations, satisfied that the fund has a sound track record, sound history of profits, good investments and management, then it is clearly an investment superior to a U.S. investment company with comparable attributes. And if from the gross profits point of view the two are equivalent, tax considerations weigh heavily in favor of the offshore fund in view of the advantages of growth in whole dollars and the larger investment possibilities of offshore funds.

Numbered Bank Accounts? Investment in offshore funds is the lowest grade of possible involvement with tax havens. The next step "up" is putting money in confidential, or numbered, bank accounts. This is usually combined with out-and-out tax evasion. Needless to say, such a combination is illegal and very risky. Beware!

Incorporation. The next level of tax haven involvement requires that the investor incorporate in a tax haven or establish a trust in one. Trusts are good if the money is intended not for oneself but for his loved ones. If, however, the objective is to advantage oneself rather than his heirs, what is needed is a corporation. This opens up a very wide range of possibilities. We will discuss some basic and important ones, but not the whole range of opportunities; that would require a volume in itself.

The simplest possibility, and the one that most investors are likely to be interested in, is a holding company. A holding company is a company that is not directly involved in trade or production; rather, it deals in investments in other companies. It makes it possible to direct funds into investments that produce passive income—rent, dividends, royalties, interest on bonds and deposits, etc. The advantage in transferring one's investment portfolio to a tax haven corporation (whether a holding company or some other variety of investment company) is that the income derived from these investments will not be taxed as part of personal income, or, if incorporation is in the U.S., as corporate income. No such U.S. tax liabilities exist for the tax haven corporation.

However, there are three kinds of tax liabilities to be dealt with in transfering a portfolio to a haven company. It is these three kinds of liabilities that make the use of a haven a more sophisticated operation than just a simple act of creating a company in a haven and transferring investments to it.

The first of these is *U.S. withholding tax.* This liability exists to the extent that investments indicate the United States as the source of his income. If the investments are the property of a corporation registered in a no-tax haven, 30 percent of the gross income from U.S. sources would be lost to the withholding tax. Clearly, since a holding company has no real costs of operation (apart from fairly low maintenance costs), this means that the no-tax corporation brings income down into a 30 percent bracket—quite an improvement, but not a total remedy.

One way to improve on this is to use a low-tax, double-taxation-agreement haven for incorporation. In this case, the agreement would usually serve to reduce the withholding tax to 15 percent, and then the low local haven tax would be imposed on the remaining 85 percent after allowable deductions. Local taxes in the low-tax, double-taxation-agreements considered in part two of this book (the Netherlands Antilles, Barbados, and the British Virgin Islands) total at most 15 percent on the net. Thus, at worst, one's tax bracket would be 27 percent (in the BVI, the U.S. withholding tax is credited against the local tax, canceling it out; see chapter nine). Even this can be improved on if a second company in a no-tax haven is involved.

This two-company setup might work this way: If Company A is established in a low-tax, double-taxation-agreement haven and derives income from the U.S., and if Company B is in a no-tax haven, Company A could, in principle, lease some property from B and pay rent to it. Since the lease agreement is, in effect, between the investor (under the guise of Company A) and himself (under the guise of Company B), he can make it rather expensive for A to get the lease. A could even be in the "unfortunate" position of having all its gross profit (85 percent of the U.S.–source revenue) paid out as expenses to cover the very uneconomical lease with greedy B. Such a maneuver is legally chancy because the parties involved are within "an arm's length" of each other, but let us say it works. The money reaches B. There is usually no withholding tax between the country of A and that of B, and there are no local taxes on B. Thus, American withholding tax has been reduced to 15 percent (or even 5 percent in some cases), local taxes have been reduced or canceled out, and the tax rate has become about 15 percent.

Another advantage of such a two-tier structure is that it is able to bypass both Subpart F provisions and the requirement of double-taxation agreements for information exchange between the IRS and the local tax department of the country of A. This can be done by the following sequence of steps: (1) The investor incorporates Company A and reports this to the IRS. (2) A incorporates Company B. (3) B makes a lease deal with A. (4) B has been incorporated by a foreign (nonresident alien) legal entity and thus need not be reported to the IRS. (5) The investor pays his Subpart F income tax or, better yet, the tax on his dividend income derived from A. (6) All the "meat" of his profit accumulates in B. There is no legal requirement to report anything about B, including its profits, which it reinvests. A owns B, and the investor owns A. Through A he controls B and decides what it is to do with its funds.

This last, control, factor is not relevant when the investor files his tax returns. If, in the unlikely event the IRS somehow finds out about B, classifies it as a "foreign controlled corporation" or a "foreign controlled holding corporation," and demands that the investor pay taxes on its undistributed profits on the strength of Subpart F, he will have to do so for one year—until he disbands B and creates a similar outfit. But no tax evasion has been involved because the investor (1) duly reported all foreign corporations (Company A) he has been involved in as an incorporator, stockholder, director, or officer, and (2) he has reported both his personal taxable income and the income of all the foreign corporations (again, A) the IRS inquired about in order to assess his Subpart F liabilities, if any. True, he did not volunteer information about B, but there is no legal requirement for him to do so.

The above outlined approach is at best quasi-legal. It involves concealment of information that, had it been available to the IRS, may have made the investor's calculated tax burden greater. But it seems to be within the *letter* of the law, though perhaps barely so.

A more complex (and more secure) version of this approach might have Company B formed by a local trust company in B's haven country and its shares "owned" by nominees who have private contracts with the investor, valid under the laws of the land of B, to the effect that they will vote in stockholders' meetings of B as the investor instructs. The investor then instructs the nominees to decide that B will never distribute dividends and that it will reinvest all its profits, or that it will cover all his expenses as an "honored guest" when he visits the land of B, or what have you. In this case, the investor is technically neither directly nor indirectly a stockholder of B. The company is owned and run by local citizens of the land of B, who happen to have a private local contract with the investor concerning their actions as stockholders in B.

Is this all fully legal? It is very hard to say. The "evasion/avoidance" distinction is more than a little vague and open to interpretation. The IRS could claim that the investor indirectly exerted control over Company B, though this would likely require a very strong case to prove the investor's control over the nominees' voting behavior at stockholders' meetings. It is possible that the whole affair might be construed by U.S. courts to be a case of foreign "corruption" outside the judicial authority of the United States—and then again, maybe not. Such things are very "iffy," and although the chances of this kind of arrangement coming to light are quite slim, the potential penalties are grave. The worries associated with it may well not be worth the potential gain. It all depends on the peculiarities and particular circumstances of the individual investor.

The second tax liability involves Subpart F income. There are more "legal" types of arrangements than those discussed above to take care of this. These involve proper patterning of stock ownership and income structure. To understand these two factors, observe that a "controlled foreign corporation" is defined for Subpart F purposes as a foreign corporation that is controlled from the U.S. (*control* meaning majority of shares of ownership), that derives income mainly from passive sources, that is engaged in "trade or business" in the U.S., and that deals with "related persons" (other companies that could be shown to have the same basic ownership, however camouflaged).

We have already indicated that a double-tier corporate arrangement *seems* to escape the first requirement. This is open to question, however, because a court could interpret *control* in a "liberal" sense, extending it to mean indirect methods of control.

The desired result might be obtained without the complexity and expense of a double tier by distributing stock ownership in the haven company as follows: 49 percent to the U.S. investor and 51 percent to a non-American, with whom the U.S. investor may have a private, foreign contract that requires him to vote as his American mentor directs. Again, it is not clear what may happen should such a setup be discovered. It is all a matter of what will prevail—the loophole-ridden letter of the law or its strangling "spirit."

There is still another approach that might serve, the proper patterning of company income. This may require that an increase in tax haven involvement from creating a mere instrument to hold a portfolio to using the haven corporation as a basis for real business activity. If the passive income of the company is at most 30 percent of its gross, the rest being derived from manufacturing, farming, mining, fishing, sales, or services, if the "securities"-generated income is at most 39 percent, and if the corporation performs genuine services for what reasonably could be claimed to be "unrelated persons," the "income pattern" should be right.

Note the use of the word *should*. Despite all the care in the world to meet the letter of the Subpart F guidelines, the IRS still could go after a setup like this and possibly make its case stick. The definition of what constitutes a controlled foreign corporation is far from precise, since "control," "trade in the United States," and "related persons" are ambiguous terms subject to interpretation by the IRS and the courts for their application. Attempting to predict what the tax collectors and judges might do is more than a little difficult. There have even been cases in which judges have ruled that the Constitution cannot be relied upon as a legal defense in tax cases!

The third kind of tax liability one must consider is that which his heirs might have to pay if he operates only with corporations. Even if he merely owns the stock of a corporation that merely owns the stock of another corporation that makes, accumulates, reinvests, and increases tax-free profits, there is something in his title (stock) potentially subject to estate taxes, inheritance duties, and so on.

Trusts. The answer to this problem could be a tax haven trust. This will be developed more fully in chapter five. For now, here are the highlights of this approach: (1) The investor establishes his trust *now,* thereby alienating the property from his estate. (2) He uses all legal means of transferring his assets to the trust without incurring gift taxes. (3) He transfers assets directly to the foreign trust only if they constitute proceeds from sales recently completed on which all due income taxes have been paid, thus eliminating both the excise duty of 35 percent and the need to pay personal income tax on the annual profits of the tax portion of these proceeds. (4) He guarantees that the trustee is a non-American, the trust deed is legalized outside the United States, and all trust assets are located outside the U.S. The trust deed should be irrevocable, otherwise the IRS would not consider the arrangement to be a trust.

The investor's beneficiaries may have to pay income tax on the benefits the trust would ultimately pay them, but they can choose between two "throwback" methods for doing so. They can pay taxes on the assumption that they received their proportional part of the trust income during each of the years the trust has been in existence. For example, if the trust made a profit of $10,000 in 1979, it starts paying benefits to John in 1980, and John is entitled to 10 percent of the trust's payout, he can pay taxes as if an extra $1,000 (10 percent of $10,000) were added to his *1979* income.

The other throwback method that trust beneficiaries can select is the "short-cut" approach. This involves averaging the trust's income over the years of its existence. If, say, the trust existed for fifty years and made a total net income (tax-free because it is in a haven) of $1 million, its average annual income is $20,000. Compute the annual income for each beneficiary according to his proportionate entitlement to trust benefits. If John is entitled to 10 percent of the trust's payout, his annual entitlement is $2,000 (10 percent of the $20,000 average). Add these annual entitlements to John's income for each of the three preceding years. In our example, he would add $2,000 to each year's income. (4) Compute the extra income tax to be paid for each of these three years, average this extra tax over the three years, and multiply the average obtained by the number of years the trust made profits (fifty in this case). The answer derived in this last step is John's full tax bill on his trust income.

As can be readily seen, trusts can reduce the tax load on one's heirs. A trust holding the shares of a tax haven corporation that accumulates profits tax-free can avert all estate duties and the like. A trust combined with a double-tier corporate arrangement using a low-tax, double-taxation-agreement haven and a no-tax haven, as described above, can provide some immunity against withholding tax, Subpart F tax, estate tax, death tax, and probate. Needless to say, such arrangements are costly. However, if appreciable savings over many years are involved, the cost may be more than justified.

Thus far, we have discussed methods that might be used to avoid tax liabilities on a portfolio of investments. This is in line with our basic premise that the major use of tax havens should not be to defend against taxes on primary income—that accruing to one from his work—but against taxes on secondary income from investments. This is on the assumption that most people do not wish to change their basic life plan and lifestyle in order to reduce taxes, but merely to reduce the tax burden on an already established life pattern.

However, tax considerations and business considerations are really inseparable, once the basic departure point is the maximization of money one can use, and not gross profit or minimal taxes. Tax havens open up certain possibilities not only for better general investment (offshore funds) or tax-secured investment (foreign holding companies and/or trusts). They also offer active possibilities for moneymaking as bases for international trade and production that are not only untaxed but relatively unregulated and uncontrolled. The legal basis for such activities is quite the same as that discussed above with respect to transferring an investment portfolio to a tax haven corporation, trust, or a multitiered combination of more than one tax haven legal entity. And the specific possibilities are rather large.

The first of these is financial activities. One can establish a finance company, or even a bank, in some havens, alone or with partners. In some havens, the local regulations on finance companies and banks are surprisingly lax compared to those in the United States. Most Americans believe that only a Rockefeller can consider starting a bank. Yet, in certain havens, this is possible with relatively limited funds. Further, banks tend to be more secure against Subpart F problems than other haven entities.

Finance companies are usually even easier to establish, and no less immune to Subpart F, than banks. Nice profits are possible in the international money market, especially those connected with intercurrency exchange deals, utilizing the day-to-day fluctuations, as well as the differences in relative values of currencies from place to place. Clearly, this is no mere pastime involvement; it may become a thrilling full-time activity.

Another enterprise, requiring substantial capital, is a haven-based insurance company, to insure one's own business. This is called a "captive" insurance company. Because this is something few people can do, we will indicate the advantages of such a company only in passing. The premiums a business pays to an insurance company are tax-deductible expenses in the United States, and net *profit* in the haven locality where the insurance company is incorporated. The premiums may be, for the same kind of damages and other losses, less than what one would have to pay an American company, which has to pay taxes on its income and so has to inflate its premiums. And a business can be insured against risks for which there are no actuarial (statistical) tables and for which ordinary insurers offer no coverage; this would provide a sound business reason for having a captive insurance company.

But back to more realistic possibilities. Manufacturing in a haven, using the low-wages, nonunion, no-regulations situation, and selling the product through another company in the U.S., there would be taxes to be paid on profits from distribution of the product in the United States, but the profits as a manufacturer, accounted as export profits of the haven manufacturing company, would accumulate tax free. Of course, being a very hard-bargaining exporter and a very stupid importer would cause a majority of the total profits to be made by the haven manufacturing company. If Subpart F becomes a problem (because of deals between "related persons" and involvement in "trade or business" with the U.S.), the products can be exported only to foreign countries other than the United States.

If the manufacturing company has no deals with anyone in the U.S., and so has no Subpart F liabilities, one can make part of his relations with it "official," reducing his U.S. taxable income by the commissions, dividends, management fees, and whatever other intangible services he can come up with, provided him by the haven company. Thus, a haven corporation can be both a tool for reducing U.S. net taxable income as well as a basis for multinational operations. In some havens, the local government, eager for foreign investments, may even help by providing subsidies, privileges, low-interest loans, and more.

How about shipping? A shipping line based in Panama or Liberia, both noted tax havens, would be immune from any U.S. taxes if its ships did not enter American internal waters, and would be free of the many complex and costly regulations concerning personnel, safety, etc., imposed by the United States.

Another possibility, the last we will discuss but by no means the last one available, is to extend services (technical, managerial, engineering, architectural, scientific, and so on) through a haven corporation on an international basis outside the United States. If, say, a Venezuelan company were provided with engineering designs and bills in the name of the haven corporation, the deal would be strictly foreign. The haven company would be able to accumulate professional fees on a tax-free basis.

So tax haven involvement can range from the minimum of buying offshore funds through using haven corporate and trust entities to reduce taxes on investment returns and eliminate death duties to full-time involvement in international business activities. An investor's background, occupation, professional training and qualifications, interests, concerns, disposition, economic situation, etc., will determine what he does with tax havens. Only a cool and detailed inspection of the specific situation, with the aid of competent professional advice, can determine what precise approach should be followed.

This book does not offer a do-it-yourself kit of forms to finalize incorporation or trust formation abroad. Such a quicky deal is as dangerous as performing a kidney operation on your own wife by using a do-it-yourself surgical manual. The manual may be all right, but who in his right mind would risk it? In principle, a "Do-It-Yourself Tax Haven Manual" is possible; whatever expertise professionals have in the field could be formulated in precise and complete detail. However, such a book, if honestly and competently put together, would be gigantic, and would amount to a combination of relevant legal training, relevant accountancy training, and much detailed information about the tax and corporate laws of a multitude of countries. The time required for a layman to digest such a manual would be worth more than the price of good professional advice. Trying to avoid both such a detailed manual and the costs of professional advice, using a short-cut approach, would be cheaper in the short run—and much, much more costly in the long run.

So anyone interested in pursuing any of the possibilities presented here should definitely get in touch with the best professional advisors he can afford before going into action. It will mean risks, expense, and hard work, but properly done, it could be very much worth it.

FIVE

Tax Haven Corporations and Trusts

The essence of using tax havens for tax reduction purposes is the creation of legal entities that have these characteristics: (1) They are separate from their creator in a fashion guaranteeing that the income they derive from their assets cannot be considered part of his income. (2) They "reside" in countries where the tax situation is much better than in the United States. (3) An investor can control them and their assets and income as he pleases, without either U.S. tax or debt liabilities.

Such business entities exemplify the basic idea of separating ownership and control. Once one's portfolio has been vested in such an entity, he no longer has title to it. But since he has title to stock in the company, he has the power to make decisions about the ways its assets are used.

There are two basic forms of such entities: the corporation and the trust. We will discuss both in turn, because all the countries that we will later consider as possible tax havens allow at least one form or the other; all of them allow corporations, and some allow trusts. (There are additional kinds of business entities available in Liechtenstein.) At this juncture, it is very important that the nature of corporations and trusts and all the related concepts defined by reference to them be clearly understood.

Corporations. Contrary to popular belief, corporations are not necessarily "big" companies, though there are some size characteristics that are relevant to the decision of whether or not to incorporate. Below a certain asset value, incorporation is usually not worthwhile.

But first, just what is a corporation? To understand this, it is important to reflect on the way the corporate form of business enterprise first came into being. The initial motivation for forming corporations had nothing to do with taxes; rather, it had to do with debts. If one is, say, a grocer who owns his own store, any loan he takes out to buy stock for his shelves is his *personal* loan, his personal debt. The security for the loan, the assets that can be taken away from him and sold to cover the loan and repay the debtor, is all the grocer's personal assets, everything he owns. If he fails to repay a loan taken out for business purposes, his debtors can claim his TV set, house, car—everything. This means that if one runs a business as a personal property, he has unlimited debt liability; the business' debts are its owner's debts.

Because of this, many persons felt the need to separate business from their personal lives and to defend their personal property from the adverse consequences of business mistakes and failures. The corporation was the answer. Incorporation was, in effect, a declaration like this: "If you give my business a loan, you should know in advance that, in case the business fails to repay you, you have recourse only to what the business owns, not what I personally own." In other words, the formation of a corporation is the creation of a new "legal person" insofar as liabilities are concerned. This legal person can assume its own debts and acquire its own assets. The assets may derive from the individual who establishes the corporation, and he then becomes liable for the debts of the company, but only to the extent of the assets expressly transferred to the corporation or committed to such a transfer. An act of government, the registration of the corporation, makes valid this "legal personification" and defends those with interests in the company from invasions of business debtors into their private lives.

At first glance, incorporation seems to be nothing but a legal trick to escape full responsibility for bad decisions. But it has fuller significance and justification when partnerships are concerned. If, say, one is a partner with his neighbor in a small, unincorporated repair shop, both partners are fully liable for the business' debts. If the neighbor runs off with all the company cash, his unfortunate partner would still be liable for all the debts incurred by the business.

Suppose one is a passive partner, having lent money to someone to open a shop saying, "I don't want to be a creditor, but a partner. Fifty percent of the profits will be mine after a salary for you is deducted from the profits." Sometime later it is discovered that the active partner has incurred debts beyond the value of the assets of the shop and his own personal property, leaving the passive partner —who had nothing to do with running the business —with the responsibility of covering the remaining debts out of his own pocket.

And what about many partners in an enterprise? There seems to be full business justification for becoming a partner with a very small percentage interest in a company, without any active participation in running it but with a percentage of the profit proportional to the original investment. But such an arrangement is quite unfeasible if one has full liability for the company's debts. Who would want to run the risk of having a $100 investment suddenly become a liability of $1 million as a consequence of someone else's blunders?

Since it seemed that economic growth required such investment partnerships, and since most people would be reluctant to take part in them if it involved unlimited liability for the partnership's debts, the idea of incorporation became widely accepted. It answered a need. Its essence was that instead of being a partner in the title of a business property (and thus a proportional direct owner of the business' assets), one owned stock. Stocks are certificates of partial ownership in a corporation. The corporation is a legal person that owns its own assets and has its own liabilities. Owning the stock of the corporation does not mean owning its assets. The corporation has title to these. The stockholder has title to his stock.

The value of the stock may have been printed on it (par value); it might be, say, $20. This means only that this number was printed on the stock certificate, and that if one went through all the certificates ever issued in the name of the company, added up all the figures of par value printed on them, and got a total of $20,000 (the *authorized capital* of the company), the proportion of the ownership in the corporation represented by one share would be one-thousandth.

Par value is not necessarily what would be paid for the stock. In principle, a buyer could pay a "percentage" of, say, 10 percent of par. This would mean that he could pay $2 and owe the company $18. If everybody bought stock at the same percentage, this would mean that the corporation would start off with a *paid-up capital* of $2,000, 10 percent of its authorized capital. If tomorrow our example company got into heavy debt and declared bankruptcy, the liquidator, whether a private individual or the government, would inspect the company books and find that it has $2,000 of paid-up capital and that the stockholders owe the company $18,000. The stockholders' debt is the company's asset, and it has to be called in to pay off the corporation's debts. But the debtors cannot make claims against the stockholders beyond the amount they owe the company.

Some stock has no par value. In such cases, each certificate represents a part of the total ownership of the corporation equal to that represented by any other. Even so, legal requirements for a minimum of authorized capital and, usually, paid-up capital apply everywhere. Clearly, such minima are necessary; nobody would give a loan to a corporation if there were no clue to at least its authorized capital.

A stockholder's percentage of ownership in a corporation equals the number of shares he holds divided by the total issued. The corporation may have a fixed authorized capital or, in some countries, a variable one. Say it can vary between $10,000 and $50,000. It may start, then, with 100 shares of $100 par value each. Each such share would then equal one percent control of the company. But then the company could expand its capital base by selling new shares up to the limit of $50,000. A $100 share would then represent only 0.2 percent control.

Another important distinction concerning shares of corporate stock is that between *registered* and *bearer* shares. A registered share has the name of its current owner printed on the certificate and in the official corporation record (the shareholders ledger). The record of registered shares is open to official inspection, and the owners of such stock are easily identified. A registered share thus has obvious drawbacks when privacy is important.

A bearer share belongs to whoever physically holds it; there is no name on it, and its sale is not logged anywhere. The sale of registered shares is always recorded and, depending on the corporation, may require the agreement of other shareholders. Bearer shares can be bought and sold in complete privacy without any third-party interference.

Bearer shares are not allowed in some tax havens. They open the way to certain quasi-legal tricks. For example, suppose Peter incorporates a company in a tax-haven and represents its ownership by one bearer share. Before he declares his annual income and reports his ownership of a foreign corporation pursuant to Subpart F regulations, he gives the bearer share to a friend, Paul. (This may involve paying a gift tax to make the deal fully legal.) Peter turns in his report to the IRS. Paul now gives the bearer share back to Peter and then turns in his tax report. He has no need to report the net income of the foreign corporation because at the time he worked up his report he did not own it. Peter did not have to report an interest in the company because at the time he did his report he did not own it either.

All this may seem more than a little fishy. How legal is it? It seems to meet the letter of the law, but what about the spirit of the law? Only a judge can divine that.

Another problem with bearer shares is that they can be stolen, and the owner has no means of proving ownership. In addition, unlike registered shares, which can be purchased at a percentage, bearer shares usually must be paid for in full.

It is possible to have the "best of both worlds" by buying registered shares at a percentage and having them registered in the name of a proxy. This reduces the capital requirements while at the same time providing privacy and security. A private contract can be arranged with the proxy that binds him to follow the real owner's instructions in all his actions as a stockholder. A proxy can be a real individual or an institution. Corporation A can hold stock in Corporation B, serving as a holding company. Holding companies are very popular because they can, if they are foreign corporations, release their owners from registered ownership; they can be used to absorb and reinvest returns on the shares they hold in buying new shares without U.S. tax liabilities; and they can be established in many countries with very low local tax liabilities, even if there are heavy local taxes on other types of corporations.

This leads us to the issue of control of corporations in general, which is an important one. A corporation is a legal person; while being, in essence, a documentary fiction, it must simulate somehow the faculties and capacities of a real person. It must have the ability to evaluate its past actions and its present circumstances, to reach policy decisions in light of this information, to implement them in specific everyday decisions, and to commit itself contractually. A real person does all these things. A corporation must have a legal anatomy that allows it to simulate the psychological anatomy of a real person. This dictates the traditional structure and nature of a corporation.

The basic existence of a corporation usually derives from two documents, the *articles of incorporation* and the *articles of association* (by-laws). The articles of incorporation are prepared by the lawyer who represents the corporation. They must include certain information about the newly born pseudo-person: (1) *Its name* (including an indication of its status as a corporation such as "Inc." [incorporated], "Co." [company], or whatever else local conventions associate with corporate status). The name must not be the same as that of an already existing corporation and must not be misleading according to local conventions. Some countries, for instance, forbid companies to use their national names as part of a corporate name. (2) *Its registered address.* This is required to make possible communication with the corporation. (3) *Its objects and aims.* Usually, these are stated broadly, but they must be so stated as not to allow any reason for suspicion that the corporation is formed to promote illegal or immoral aims. (4) *Its capitalization.* There is country-to-country variability concerning this requirement. It usually pertains to authorized capital, the paid-up capital, the nature of shares (par value, no par value, number, registered, bearer, premium, no premium). This stipulation is usually required to be backed up by some officially acceptable proof (such as a bank account record) that the minimum paid-up capital requirements have been met by cash or by assets whose provable value adds up to the minimum. (5) *A statement that the company is a limited liability organization.*

Apart from these general requirements, local laws differ. In some cases, names of persons associated with the corporation must also be mentioned, with their addresses: shareholders, ultimate-beneficiary share-owners (in the cases where shares are held by proxies), directors, officers. Other countries may require a specification of the span of time the corporation is supposed to exist before liquidation. Sometimes the articles of association are required to be a part of the articles of incorporation. The articles of incorporation are usually approved and confirmed by a government official, the "Registrar of Companies" or something comparable. Most often, but not always, an announcement of the formation of a new corporation is required to be published in some official government gazette.

The articles of association usually must also be submitted to the government registrar. These articles represent the basic terms of a corporation's structure and direction. There are variations from country to country on the requirements. In some places the local law is rigid and detailed; in others it indicates broad outlines and certain specific restrictions. Thus the law may require that each corporation have a board of directors and that at least one director reside in the country where incorporation takes place. However, the law may leave the number of directors open. This, of course, is a mere illustration.

Some uniform features of corporations, following from the essential nature of a corporation as a fictitious person that simulates a real person, are:

Stockholders' Meeting. This is the "ultimate authority" of the corporation. There is usually a requirement that it meet annually, and sometimes there is a requirement that it have a quorum of a certain percentage of the shares outstanding. In this meeting all stockholders are allowed to participate and, usually, to vote, with one vote per share. Sometimes, however, there are nonvoting shares, sold as such.

The annual meeting has to discuss and approve certain things by majority decision: (1) The business actions of the corporation in the preceding year as represented by its declared annual accounts of both profit and loss and its assets and liabilities. The correctness of these documents usually has to be certified by a separate body of auditors or accountants. Disapproval of such reports by the majority of the stockholders is similar to a parliamentary no-confidence vote. It is an expression of dissatisfaction with the management of the company. (2) Policy decisions on future business actions. Trends of possible company developments have to be approved, as well as the manner in which the net profit of the company (after deduction of both expenses and taxes) is to be divided. What dividend will the shareholders receive? How much will go for investment in company growth? How much will be kept in bank reserves? (3) Personnel decisions. Should the president, secretary, and treasurer be retained or replaced? Should the auditors continue to be the same? Are the directors satisfactory? (4) Constitutional issues. Should the articles of association be modified within the limit of the law? Should the quorum requirements be changed? The annual meeting is chaired by an elected chairman. His position is a distinct one in the company structure.

Board of Directors. While the annual meeting constitutes the "parliament" of the corporation, the articles of association also specify requirements for the "cabinet," the board of directors. How many directors? How are they appointed? How are they replaced? How many times do they meet? And so on. In general, the board is supposed to make decisions on the issues that are too specific for the general meeting to discuss but which are beyond the day-to-day responsibility of the company management.

Corporate officers. Another cabinetlike institution, sometimes part of the board of directors, is the group of corporate officers—the president, the secretary, the treasurer, etc. These individuals usually have the right to represent the company to third parties, to negotiate and make commitments in its name. This means they can put it into debt, and stipulations may be made as to whether they can do this separately or only in common. The local law may specify an annual minimum of officers' and directors' meetings, even sometimes demanding a specific location for them; it may stipulate whether the directors have to be at the meetings in person or whether they can be represented by proxies. The law may also (and usually does) require a corporation to keep records of proceedings and decisions in such meetings, a book of minutes that, in some places, must be open to public and/or official inspection.

Auditors. The last body usually required is the auditors, who are required to inspect the company's bookkeeping and verify the correctness of annual accounts. These are not usually employees or directors of the corporation but an outside firm.

The legal structure of a corporation is distinct, of course, from its operational structure. It may have branches, divisions, departments, etc., headed by managers or executives who may or may not be members of the board of directors and may act separately or collectively as the articles of association may specify explicitly or as the directors or officers dictate.

Now, this looks a formidable structure, and one may wonder if having so many employees may not cost more than the taxes to be minimized through incorporation. But all this vast structure need not be more than a tissue of technicalities if incorporation is accomplished in a tax haven. If the local law requires three initial incorporators, these can be supplied, for a reasonable fee, by the local law firm that handles the incorporation. These proxies can then either turn over their shares to the "real incorporator" after incorporation or continue to act on his behalf under a private contract. Similarly, the general meeting of stockholders can in some cases be no more than a meeting with of the single majority stockholder in front of the bathroom mirror, with minutes duly recorded, of course. If this is not good enough for the local law, a real local annual stockholders' meeting can be arranged by the corporate legal representative in the haven, with proxies provided for moderate fees.

The same sort of arrangements can be made to cover all requirements for local corporate officers and the like. The "ultimate owner" can run the company as he pleases, with all the legally formidable structure and rituals carried out by proxies.

Returning to the essential aspects of corporations, it should be remembered that the corporate legal form came into being for business purposes, not tax purposes. Corporations were invented to encourage capital investment in the form of ownership with limited debt liability. Since corporations are legal persons, government approval is required to form them, and corporation laws, quite similar all over the world but with important place-to-place variations, have been enacted, establishing government control over the formation and operation of corporations. Moreover, since corporations, as legally acknowledged persons, make possible all kinds of sophisticated fraud, governments encourage their formation. This claim may seem strange, but nonetheless it is true. The existence of corporations enhances government's role of "defender of the innocent" against the "robber barons." Very complex corporation laws, requiring publication of annual corporate accounts and records, independent accounting, forbidding deals of "no less than arm's length" between two corporations with the same or virtually the same ownership of certain kinds, and so on, are justified by reference to the opportunities for corporate mischief.

On the other hand, corporations require special tax treatment, to avoid killing the goose that lays the golden egg. They cannot be taxed progressively, as individuals are, because the "justification" for progressive taxation of individuals does not apply. If an individual has a very large income, he is "too rich," and the soak-the-rich mentality of modern welfare statism makes progressive taxation popular. But even a huge corporation with large gross profits can be owned by thousands of "little men." Progressive corporate taxation would wipe out the little guys' profits—hardly a politically popular consequence—and would discourage investment in corporations. Consequently, with but two exceptions, corporate income taxes everywhere are assessed at flat rates, in most cases 40–50 percent of net profits. The exceptions are, of all places, Switzerland and Liechtenstein. In these two nations, corporate-tax brackets are determined by the ratio between profit and authorized capital. For example, $100,000 made on an authorized capital of $1 million, a 10 percent yield, would be taxed at a higher rate than the same dollar profit on an authorized capital of $10 million, a one percent yield.

The fact that corporate taxes are flat-rate taxes means that incorporation can be used to reduce tax burdens by alienating personal sources of income to a corporation. This may be a good idea, and it is a major reason for incorporation in a tax haven that has no or very low corporate taxes.

In sum, here is what a tax haven corporation can do for a shrewd investor: It can alienate returns on investments from personal income, and thus save them from crippling U.S. tax rates. Even if the investments are in the United States, a tax haven corporation can reduce the total tax on them, sometimes, with a proper setup, to as low as 5 percent. The profits can then be reinvested to grow in whole dollars. If these fast-growing savings are repatriated to the U.S. as dividends or as capital gains on the liquidation of the corporation, the investor will have to pay U.S. taxes. Shrewd investors live off the income from their work and keep reinvesting the tax haven profits abroad, to be tapped later upon retirement or to be passed on to heirs.

Concerning the matter of inheritance, if the money is returned to the United States while the investor is still alive, there will be a tax penalty in the form of high income or capital gains taxes and, at the investor's death, estate taxes and probate duties. If the tax haven company survives the investor, its stock is part of his estate and is subject to estate taxes and probate in the U.S. In both cases, if the tax haven investment is principally intended to benefit heirs, a tax haven trust is called for.

Trusts. Like corporations, trusts were originally spawned by nontax considerations. A careful father, suspicious of his frivolous and careless son, yet still affectionately concerned for his future, would decide not to bequeath the whole of his accumulated wealth directly to his son. Rather, he would set up a trust, a contract (the trust deed, or instrument) between himself (the trustor) and a trustee. The trustee would be somebody who could be counted on to responsibly manage and disburse the trust assets; he could be a personal friend, the family lawyer, or a professional trust company. The trustee would agree to manage the trust fund, or assets, which are thereby alienated from the founder's property and become a legally distinct entity, like a corporation, with its own assets and liabilities.

The trustee would invest the assets according to his own discretion within the limits of the provisions of the trust deed. He would then, after a period specified in the trust deed and in conformance with pertinent legal requirements, start paying the trust beneficiary (the son) a regular sum as specified in the trust deed. This payout might be subject to certain conditions laid down by the trustor: the son gets the money only if, say, he is married before he turns thirty, or only if he refrains from drinking cherry brandy, or what have you. The money distributed to the beneficiary would include both the return on the investment of the trust principal, the original sum constituting the assets of the trust, as well as, gradually, portions of the principal itself. The trust would be legally required to terminate at some point, when all funds, principal, and return on principal, have been distributed to the beneficiary, less, of course, management expenses incurred by the trustee.

As you can see, a trust serves a role similar to that of a will, with these additional advantages: (1) It can be separate from one's will and thereby maintain the secrecy of certain heirs who it would be socially inconvenient to acknowledge in a publicly read will.

(2) It allows for the separation of some assets from one's property for inheritance purposes before death, and these assets are thereby immune to further business liabilities incurred by the trustor. This way, especially if the trust is *irrevocable* (the trustor being debarred under the trust deed from canceling it and reabsorbing the trust assets) and the trustor or his wife is not a beneficiary, money can be guaranteed to the trustor's loved ones without threat of loss through bankruptcy or other reverses. His creditors would have no access to the trust assets, since they would be separated from his estate. (3) It allows for competent professional management of the trust assets. (4) It allows the trustor to determine what aspects of the beneficiary's life he wants to encourage (or discourage) by allocating benefits for certain specified purposes. This contrasts with a will, which determines transfer of ownership, but which can establish no control over what is done with the transferred assets after the transfer is made. (5) It allows avoidance of laws that limit the right to decide how a legacy will be divided.

The major disadvantages of a trust are, of course, irrevocability and the chance of trustee abuse of trust assets. The latter can be avoided by careful formulation of the trust deed and careful trustee selection. In the case of professional trust companies, any temptation to abuse trustee powers is strongly moderated by the need to maintain a good professional reputation.

A minor disadvantage is that legal tradition generally requires that a trust have a fixed, or "upward-bounded," perpetuity period, at the end of which the trust assets must be completely disbursed to beneficiaries. The perpetuity period is variously defined in different countries.

It is important to understand that trusts are quite different from corporations. Usually, they need not be publicly recorded. A legal contract, combined with proper separation of the trust fund from the trustor's assets, establishes the trust. The contract, moreover, is peculiar in that (1) those who have rights to sue on the basis of it (the beneficiaries, who are entitled to sue the trustee if he violates the provisions of the trust deed in a manner that harms them) are not parties to the contract, (2) one party to the contract, the trustor, is usually debarred by law from any official right to intervene in the management of the trust, and (3) the trustee, who has full power to manage and distribute trust assets, cannot have any personal interest in the trust.

This peculiar legal structure, with the infinite possibilities for variation it allows, is a historical development in the common law tradition. Common law is peculiar in that it arose from a tradition of concrete cases, established in courts by reference to precedent rather than to statute law. It applies in the United Kingdom and its former colonies, including the United States and all Commonwealth countries. Only common law countries permit true trusts.

There exists another legal tradition, dating back to old Rome, revitalized and modernized by Napoleon in his Code Napoléon and accepted throughout continental Europe and in the new states that are former colonies of France, Germany, and others. This is the civil law tradition. It accepts as the basis for legal reasoning legal principles derived from explicit legislation. Precedent has a very limited role. While some civil law countries have enacted trust laws allowing the simulation of common law trusts within a civil law framework, it is generally advisable *not* to use such a simulacrum. It is only the rich common law tradition that guarantees beneficiaries their rights under the provisions of a trust. An artificial trust law is unlikely to capture many of the undreamt of possibilities specific cases may pose, and a judge deprived of the support of the vast common law tradition may decide in a very arbitrary manner sanctioned by the schematic, underdeveloped, officially legislated law. There are many common law tax havens in which to settle a trust, so there is no need to consider the civil law havens for this purpose. (Liechtenstein, as we will discuss later, is an important exception to this general rule.)

But what do trusts have to do with taxes? To begin with, money given to a trust when the trustor is alive (a living trust) may be subject to a gift tax, but not to heavy estate taxes and probate duties. Thus, a living trust is superior to a testamentary trust, one that is established in a will, because the latter can be established only with funds already decimated by taxes and probate. Moreover, trust income is not taxable to the trustor (unless a trust is revocable, in which case the IRS considers the trust income to be the personal income of the trustor). Nor is it taxable to the trustee, who derives no benefits from its growth (except his fees and expenses, which are tax deductible expenses of the trust). The beneficiaries, of course, cannot be taxed until they start receiving benefits. The trust itself, if established in the U.S., is subject to a flat-rate tax on its income. But a foreign trust is not subject to this tax, and so can serve to reinvest its income tax-free, growing rapidly through whole-dollar investment. Thus, a tax haven trust can do for one's heirs what a tax haven corporation can do for oneself.

In 1976 Congress cracked down on foreign trusts, those formed in tax havens to avoid taxes on trust income. A 35 percent excise duty was imposed on funds transferred to such trusts, and the trust income became taxable to the trustor in proportion to the amount of his donation to the trust. If a trustor donated 100 percent of a trust's assets, all of the trust's income would be declared part of his personal income. This legislation seemed to destroy completely the tax advantages of foreign trusts. But it didn't; there is a loophole. If a trustor makes a sale of property, declares it fully, pays income tax or capital gains tax on the proceeds, then transfers the remainder to a foreign trust, he escapes both the excise tax and the annual income tax on the profits of the trust. Under these circumstances, of course, the beneficiaries, if Americans, will still have to pay U.S. taxes on their benefits. But they can use "throwback" rules in a manner that will minimize their liability (as discussed in chapter three), and in most cases, their tax brackets will be lower than that of their benefactor, so the total tax burden is held to a minimum.

Tax haven trusts can be used in conjunction with haven corporations. Instead of owning a holding company that, in turn, holds stock and other investments, one can be a beneficiary of a trust established by a foreign holding company to hold its own stock. This and other double-tier structures are of huge importance when Subpart F provisions come into play.

Remember that trusts, unlike corporations, are almost never publicly advertised entities. No official confirmation of their creation has to be published anywhere. No audited accounts need reach anybody except the trustor and/or his beneficiaries. Such privacy allows one to decide, on the basis of whatever considerations he chooses to take into account, what information should be broadcast publicly.

SIX

Some Notes About Taxes

We have already said a lot about taxes in passing. In doing this it was assumed that the reader has at least some general familiarity with most of the concepts referred to. However, full utilization of the information in this book requires a firm grasp of the basics of taxation in the United States and in the tax haven countries. We will not go into arcane technicalities; that is what accountants and tax lawyers are for. But informed decisions based on the recommendations of lawyers and accountants cannot be made without a solid command of the basics. So, to work.

The most familiar form of taxation is the income tax. In view of the fact that legal entities, those kinds of things that can have income, spend money, sign contracts, etc., and hence pay taxes, are of two kinds, human beings and corporations (including trusts), there are two kinds of income taxes: personal and corporate.

Personal income tax is what federal, state, and—

all too often these days—local governments take from each of us as a percentage of our personal incomes. Its "skeleton" is a system of income brackets. These brackets establish varying rates of tax, varying percentages of taxpayer's income to be taxed away. The first $3,000, say, is not taxed at all. The next $1,000 is taxed 5 percent. Thus, only $50 must be paid on a $4,000 annual income, 5 percent of the fourth $1,000. Observe that while the percentage of the tax to total income is 1.25 percent, the tax bracket is 5 percent. Similarly, the fifth $1,000 may be taxed at a rate of 7 percent. Thus, on $5,000 the total tax would be $120, or 2.4 percent—much lower than the top tax bracket of 7 percent.

This concept of brackets is crucial to understanding what tax havens are all about because it makes clear what alienating income for tax bracket reduction means. If one divides an annual income of $5,000 between himself and his cat (somehow made into a respectable income-earning citizen by the IRS computers), $3,000 to himself and $2,000 to Tabby, he effectively gets $5,000 tax-free, assuming the bracket structure in the above example. This is a saving that is much more appreciated by someone with an annual gross income of $30,000 or above, which may put him in the 40 percent tax bracket with $6,000 in taxes. Divided on paper between ten people, each getting $3,000, the bracket system implies no tax at all.

Personal income tax is based on *net* income. Net income is gross income less all expenses that can be claimed as necessary to produce the gross—or at least necessary to an *attempt* to create or increase it. Thus, to take a less than serious example, if one earns $30,000 as an undertaker and spends $10,000 on futile parties intended to convince people to commit suicide after signing wills entrusting the care and burial of their bodies to him, the $10,000 can be claimed as business expenses and so reduce his taxable income to $20,000. This means, of course, that the tax is also levied at a much lower rate (bracket). What constitutes a business expense depends, in large measure, on the imagination and experience of one's accountant and on adequate documentation—receipts, canceled checks, etc. This is important to remember for some tax haven applications. One may incorporate a tax haven company that can get funds from the United States at a reduced tax rate, but which is locally taxable on its *net* income.

It is important to realize that personal income tax is only grossly determined by the brackets applicable to net income. There are further refinements, depending on the sources of income. In general, personal income derives from some or all of the following sources: wages, salary, fees for work or services; rent on property or real estate; dividends paid on investments; interest on bank deposits and corporate and government bonds; royalties on the use of patents or copyrights; and capital gains from the sale of property at a profit.

This breakdown of income sources is important for tax purposes. To begin with, capital gains are almost universally taxed separately on the basis of much more lenient scales and rates than those applying to ordinary income. Some countries do not tax capital gains at all. It is possible to channel investments in such a manner as to place all returns on the books as capital gains. Further, governments are not only interested in taking away part of our incomes as taxes. They are also interested in encouraging us to use what is left in "socially responsible" ways. Thus, they can reduce tax rates on income derived from interest paid on certain types of bonds or on certain dividends. Similarly, royalties may be taxed differently, depending on their source. In other words, the constitution of a taxpayer's income can make a big difference in his tax bill.

This means that, when making investment decisions, a businessman or investor should take into account IRS rulings on the various tax rates applicable to income from different sources. For instance, if he gets dividends from stock he holds in a company, he is taxed twice, indirectly when the company is taxed on its net profit, and directly when he is taxed on his dividend income. The tax on dividends is inevitable, if the investor personally holds the stock. The tax on corporate profits may be eliminated if the stock is in a tax haven corporation or offshore fund, because a company operating outside the U.S. cannot be reached by the IRS (with certain limited exceptions).

It is also important to realize that Americans are citizens of the only major country in the world that taxes total *worldwide* income, regardless of where in the world a taxpayer may live. And it does so on top of whatever taxes he may pay to the government of the country in which he resides, unless that country has a double-taxation agreement with the U.S. In some cases, the United States is "generous" enough to allow the taxpayer to deduct the foreign taxes from his income for U.S. tax purposes. Apart from the limited exceptions mentioned above, the only way to get around double taxation is to be an employee of a U.S. corporation working abroad for under $15,000 a year.

But, the reader may wonder, if I am living abroad, what can the IRS do to me if I simply choose to ignore it and not pay U.S. taxes? For one thing, the U.S. government can ask the country in which you live to deport you on the criminal charge of tax evasion. For another, your American passport can be revoked. Neither seems a happy prospect, though some Americans have become "tax refugees."

All of the above applies to the usual taxes imposed on personal income. Now we come to what might properly be called a penalty tax because it can amount to 66 percent of the taxable amount, and it is not imposed on anything that can be said, from an accounting point of view, to be personal income. This is the notorious Subpart F assessment, which we have already mentioned a number of times. Subpart F has been part of the tax code since 1963. Subpart F "income" is defined as the net undistributed profits of a foreign corporation in which a U.S. citizen owns a share or shares of stock, if certain conditions are satisfied. For example, if an investor owns 10 percent of a foreign corporation, under certain conditions 10 percent of the company's undistributed profit is considered to be his personal taxable income, even though he has never received one red cent of it.

Before 1963, the tax haven business was much

simpler for an American. The only thing he had to do was transfer his investments to a haven corporation. The dividends, rents, royalties, and such would thus be alienated from his income and become corporate income of the foreign company that served as his "alter ego." Of course, if the corporation sent the American investor dividend payments, these payments would be treated as part of his income for tax purposes. But the investor could direct the company to reinvest the money, making it undistributed profit, and thereby legally avoid U.S. taxes on it. It was even possible to translate personal work contracts into contracts with a foreign corporation. If, say, a dentist extracted a tooth, he would have the patient pay the foreign corporation. The company, in turn, would pay the dentist a modest salary, on which he would be taxed at low-bracket rates, while the rest of the money would accumulate abroad, tax free.

There were some limitations on this sort of thing even before 1963. Money paid from U.S. sources to outside beneficiaries, individuals, or companies, was taxed at the source at a rate of 30 percent on the gross. Thus, if our dentist made $10,000 for his foreign corporation, only $7,000 could legally reach it. Even so, in view of the fact that he could have given himself a salary from the foreign company, a salary in a bracket not exceeding 30 percent, as well as an expense account, he could still reduce his personal income tax to the point where 30 percent would be the top bracket applicable, regardless of the total size of "his" income.

The IRS was very unhappy about this situation, as one can imagine, so it pushed for changes in the tax laws to "penetrate the corporate veil," to ignore the legal presumption that a corporation was a separate legal entity with its own nationality according to its official residence. The income of foreign corporations was redefined as the personal income of its shareholders, even though it was not paid out to them as dividends. The high rate on undistributed profits was designed to "encourage" the foreign companies to distribute all profits, thereby making them personal income and eliminating the advantages of incorporation abroad. However, had this been done indiscriminately, it would have had the effect of stopping all American investment in foreign corporations. If an owner of stock in Royal Dutch Shell was taxed on his "share" in its undistributed profits, he would not remain a Royal Dutch Shell stockholder for long. To stop such overseas investment would isolate the United States economically and politically and completely eliminate the illusion that the tax laws do not substantially affect business decisions and damage free enterprise. Thus, the IRS had to formulate some regulations distinguishing those foreign corporations, called "controlled foreign corporations" or "controlled foreign holding companies," which were "evil," tax-avoidance shams, from the "good," "business-oriented" foreign corporations.

It would be pointless to try to recapitulate these regulations in detail here. They are so complex as to defy any description running fewer than 500 pages. Further, such a description would be outdated because, since the original drafting of these regulations and their approval by the Congress, many loopholes have been detected in them. There has always been a "game" here: the IRS fighting in court on the basis of *post factum* discovery of tax-avoidance schemes that defeated the IRS's already-formulated criteria to close loopholes, without at the same time disallowing all U.S. investment in foreign companies and treading on the toes of certain large and powerful vested interests; the taxpayers, defended by their lawyers and accountants, finding the new, inevitable loopholes. And so around and around.

However, there are some things one must know about Subpart F if for no other reason than to be able to understand his tax advisors. He needs to know what sort of arrangements can bypass Subpart F regulations (these were discussed in chapter three). He also needs to know the characteristics of a foreign corporation that make it a controlled foreign corporation or controlled foreign holding company. These are, roughly, as follows:

The structure of the stock ownership in the company. If fewer than 50 percent of the stockholders are U.S. citizens or residents, they cannot force the company to distribute its income. Thus, to tax them on their pro rata "share" of the undistributed profits would be to penalize them unjustly, even by IRS standards. This does not mean that exactly 50 percent is the cutoff line, but the example indicates why this consideration is relevant.

The degree of involvement of the corporation in U.S. business. Does the company "trade or do business" in the U.S.? To return to our dentist, his foreign company got all of its income from trade or business in the United States. This, together with its 100 percent American stock ownership would certainly result in its being hit as a controlled foreign corporation.

The degree to which a company derives passive income from U.S. investments. The greater the U.S. involvement of a corporation, the more likely it is to be considered "foreign" only for tax-avoidance purposes.

The overall structure of a company's income, passive or active.

Business transactions between a company and other companies that may be so similar to it in terms of ownership that they may be deemed transactions at "less than arm's length." Such transactions would be construed to be between the corporation, or the person behind it, and itself, designed to mask the real nature of the income of the company.

The business involvement of the corporation in its local habitat, or the degree to which such involvement could be claimed. If a company is, say, located in a country that grants it a special tax-exempt status that at the same time prohibits it from doing any local business, then it seems to the IRS that the only justification for its choice of location is tax avoidance, with no legitimate "business motivation" involved.

It is the basic gambit of the IRS to look for all the as yet legal means of tax avoidance and transform them, by new regulations and legislation, into illegal tax evasion. The IRS way of operating is to make one a criminal if he plans his investment portfolio and its legal organization in a manner that maximizes his net profit rather than his gross profit. Thus, a "business-motivation cover" is needed for tax-avoidance foreign corporations, because, unfortunately, the issue is not the real motivations of a tax haven incorporator, but what can be defended in court as a plausible representation of his motivations. It is therefore very important to select those havens that are active business centers so that having a company in one or more of them could be easily shown to have a sound business reason behind it.

Let us say that an investor creates a tax haven corporation and duly reports it to the IRS. He also complies with the requirements for fully reporting on his company's balance sheets and has the company pay all its profits to him as dividends, which he carefully reports and pays taxes on. His haven corporation meanwhile creates a second haven company in another country. The American investor has no personal role of any kind in this second corporation. The second company does not have to be reported to the IRS. It can hold the majority of the investment assets that the American tax-avoider wants to alienate from himself as income sources, reinvesting all profits and growing in whole dollars. Chances are that if the IRS knew about the income of the second company, it would be able to convince a judge that this income was Subpart F income. But there is no legal way for the government to require our investor to report anything about it. It is not income that must be reported as part of normal personal earnings. It does not fall under the categories of rent, wages, dividends, interest, royalties, or capital gains coming to the investor. And there is no legal requirement to inform the IRS about the existence of the second corporation because it was not created by a U.S. citizen or resident, real or corporate. It was created by a foreign corporation, which, as such, controlled or uncontrolled, has no legal obligations to the United States government.

The IRS will not demand that our investor report anything about "his" second corporation unless it somehow finds out about the company and his indirect association with it. And there is as yet no legal requirement that such information be *volunteered.* If the whole matter happens to wind up in court, our investor would have a strong defense against any tax-evasion charges: He reported everything he was legally expected to report. He paid his taxes in accordance with his reports. At worst, he would have to pay, by court order, the Subpart F income penalty he quite innocently failed to pay. But the matter could only reach court if the IRS found out about the second corporation on its own hook, having had some reason to suspect something fishy about the parent company. What might prompt such suspicions? Let us say that the first corporation, the one our investor directly created and reported, shows no profits. Obviously, the only reason for its existence (especially if it resides in some notorious tax haven such as Liechtenstein) is tax evasion. Since the first corporation does not *directly* serve such a purpose, it is clearly only a link to a second outfit which does. QED.

But suppose the first company is located in a place where there is a business motivation for its existence, and suppose, moreover, the company has some profits, which are distributed to our investor as dividends that he duly reports and pays taxes on. Then the IRS would have no good reason to suspect any tax-avoidance scheme. Further, Subpart F does not enter in because the corporation does not withhold its profits for "illegal" reinvestment in whole dollars. It pays them honestly and squarely to our investor, and he honestly and squarely reports everything and honestly and squarely pays his taxes.

Obviously, such scheming is on the fringes of legality. Our investor did not pay the taxes he would have had to pay had all the information noted above been reported, but he did not fail to report anything the law required of him. Moreover, the fact that he meticulously reported indicates his trustworthiness.

There is much less to say about corporate income tax. It is a flat-rate tax, usually levied on the net income of a corporation, irrespective of its amount. Capital gains taxes may be different in some countries and states from taxes on income from other sources, and interest, dividends, rent, and royalties may all be taxed differently from straight business profit.

Other kinds of taxes to be concerned about, whether on the federal or state level, are estate, death, and probate. To protect loved ones after death, trusts as well as certain Liechtensteinian entities can serve very well. To avoid death taxes the simple way, by giving loved ones part of an estate while one is still living, is to reckon with gift taxes. Even so, the relative rates of gift taxes and estate taxes, especially when gifts are so divided as to be outside certain critical brackets, may make this approach worthwhile exploring. A trust, though, is generally the best solution.

Another sort of tax to be especially concerned about if one wishes to save money through tax havens is withholding tax. We have already referred to it, but it is important to clarify it in detail. Withholding tax is a tax deducted at the source from incomes generated in Country A by a legal entity residing in Country B and transferred from A to B. For example, if a businessman has a tax haven corporation, X, which owns stock in American Company Y, and American Company, Y, pays X $1,000 in dividends, Y must pay $300 of that (30 percent, the U.S. withholding rate) to the IRS at the same time it makes remittance to X. X may be a genuine non-American residing in India or Belgium, but he is nonetheless subject to the withholding tax. Interest paid to non-Americans residing outside the U.S. ("nonresident aliens") on bank deposits in the United States is exempted from the U.S. withholding tax.

Withholding taxes are of importance whenever one has to consider the interaction between tax systems of different countries because he lives in Country A and derives income, directly or indirectly, from Country B. Thus, if one intends to receive dividends from his foreign corporation, or from *any* foreign corporation in which he has stock, the dividends may be reduced by the local withholding tax imposed by the country from which the funds are being sent.

Some people try to get around withholding taxes in a number of ways. One of these is to keep the dividends in a checking account in the country where the money originates and exchange a check on it with someone going there against a check on his deposit in the United States. This is usually illegal, and it may sometimes be illegal to have a foreign bank account. But, still, it is a gimmick that is hard to detect or prove without special and expensive detective work.

Suppose one doesn't want to take such risks. He may repatriate his dividends reduced by the local withholding tax. In this case, the following possibilities with respect to the IRS exist in principle: (1) The IRS considers the dividends to be part of the gross income, regardless of what the gross sum of the dividend was. It therefore taxes the dividend again, by applying the relevant tax bracket after deduction of the foreign withholding tax. (2) The IRS considers the gross dividend paid to be part of the gross income and deducts the tax withheld at the source from the total U.S. tax liability. (3) Some compromise between (1) and (2) occurs, in which the IRS construes some part of the foreign withholding tax payment as a credit against the U.S. tax bill. (4) There is a double-taxation agreement between the foreign country and the United States, consequent to which the foreign withholding tax deducted at the source is reduced and also credited against the total U.S. tax liability.

Double-taxation agreements are what to look for if one intends to invest in foreign stock from the United States. They serve to reduce the foreign withholding tax and, at the same time, to cancel the double penalty of being taxed by both the IRS and a foreign tax department. As such, these agreements have been introduced for "business" rather than tax reasons. They exist in order to encourage, or at least not discourage, American investment in foreign companies. However, double-taxation agreements become of much greater tax-minimizing importance when considered from the point of view of a foreign corporation created for the purpose of investing in the United States. Remittances to foreign corporations with such investments are normally subject to the full 30 percent withholding tax on the gross. If a corporation is located in a completely no-tax haven, an investor manages to reduce his tax liability to 30 percent. This may be quite a saving, but he may wish to pay even less.

It is here that double-taxation agreements come into play. Of course, the U.S. has no double-taxation agreements with no-tax countries. But it does have such agreements with a number of low-tax countries, agreements that are off-shoots of such arrangements the U.S. once had with their colonial mother countries. The British Virgin Islands have a double-taxation deal with the U.S. that emerged from a U.S.–U.K. agreement. The Netherlands Antilles have one that derives from the Netherlands–U.S. agreement. Both these places impose low corporate income taxes but their double-taxation agreements with the United States serve to reduce the U.S. withholding tax to, usually, 15 percent of gross.

Suppose, for purposes of illustration, that a company's net income is what remains after the 15 percent U.S. withholding tax has been deducted (85 percent of gross). The total tax on the gross would then be 27.75 percent, which is less than the standard 30 percent withholding. Clearly, the net income of a company can be reduced to much less than 85 percent of gross. And by using more than one company, the local tax can be virtually eliminated by eliminating the net profit of the local company. Moreover, certain approaches may allow reduction of the U.S. withholding tax to as low as 5 percent.

Thus, withholding tax is a curse that can be virtually neutralized by the careful exploitation of double-taxation agreements. But there is one fly in the ointment: more or less active cooperation between the tax departments of the governments involved. This is not as bad as it sounds, however, for there are plans that require nothing illegal, using only highly sophisticated, legal tax-avoidance techniques.

Let us wrap up this discussion of taxes with brief mention of a few less important, but still existent, taxes. Some countries levy annual land-value taxes. Others charge stamp duties, now almost universal taxes imposed on the value of certain officially registered documents (incorporation papers, bonds, bills of sale, IOUs, and even checks) and required for making these documents legally valid. Stamp duties must always be taken into account when dealing with a tax haven. Thus, even when we discuss no-tax havens, we do not mean places where nobody pays the government anything—more's the pity.

Now that we have the theory and practice of tax havens in hand, let us tour the best of these wonderful lands.

PART TWO:
The Tax Haven Guide

SEVEN

No-Tax Havens: Balmy Climes for Money and Man

Over the last sixty years most Americans have come to accept taxes as a basic, inalienable part of life, a sort of necessary evil. There are, however, places where there are virtually no taxes. And, wonder of wonders, most of them have good governments, "good" in the Jeffersonian sense of governing little.

These no-tax countries share some basic similarities, which are important to anyone considering forming a corporation or trust in one or another of them. These factors need to be kept in mind when forming a judgment about the likelihood of the governments of these countries violating their no-tax traditions.

All of the no-tax havens considered in this chapter are island, or archipelego, societies. Foreign invasion is most unlikely, and defense budgets are minimal to nonexistent. All have ethnically mixed populations, native peoples and white immigrants from Europe and America. They have almost no racial friction and are peaceful and nonviolent, so the "war against crime" as a major motive for taxation to support large government outlays for police activities is happily lacking.

Because of their multi-island geographies, all of these havens are free of strong central government. Where government officials have to use motorboats or even canoes to get around, their mobility is reduced and, correspondingly, so is their control. None of these countries shares the European and American notions of technologically oriented living standards. The idea that someone is "socially underprivileged" because he does not have a late-model car would seem odd to a citizen of any one of these lands, and welfare policies of the U.S. type are nonexistent and very unlikely to be introduced in the future.

Every one of these no-tax havens has a British colonial background and is a member of the British Commonwealth. While the present ultrasocialist British government is a supertaxing government, these little Commonwealth countries still operate on the "imperialist tradition" of nineteenth century British colonial policy, which typically excluded all local taxation. Moreover, the legal tradition in all of these places is that of the common law uncorrupted by socialist legislation, and the official language is English.

Finally, all of these nations, in view of their restricted land areas, depend on tourism and foreign investment for economic success. The tax haven industry is an economic necessity for each of them, and any attempt to change this by future leftist governments is improbable to say the least.

All in all, the consideration of stability is very

much in favor of these no-tax havens. They have been no-tax countries for many, many years, and they have both traditional and practical stakes in staying that way.

However, all these havens share a major disadvantage: It is very difficult to establish plausible business reasons for incorporating in them. The names Bahamas, Bermuda, and Cayman Islands are immediately suspect in the eyes of the IRS. This means that a Bahamas, Bermuda, or Cayman Islands corporation would best be formed indirectly by a corporation in another haven.

A related reason for considering these havens only in terms of a double- or multitier arrangement is the fact that one might want to derive tax-free (or tax-reduced) income from U.S. sources. No-tax countries do not have double-taxation agreements, so a corporation located in one, if directly receiving income from U.S. sources, would be subject to the full 30 percent U.S. withholding tax on gross profits. On the other hand, as a second company in a multitiered structure, not receiving income directly from the U.S. but from another corporation in a low-tax, double-taxation-agreement haven, such an outfit can be highly useful. And since these no-tax nations do not have double-taxation agreements, they have substantial privacy advantages, which are enhanced by local codes, official and unofficial, that derive from the healthy vested interest of local governments in cultivating the tax haven industry.

Before we discuss the specific no-tax countries in detail, a word about how their governments raise the little revenue they need to stay in business. The principle sources of government funds in these nations are stamp duties; legal fees, under various descriptions, payable for incorporation and legal maintenance of a company; and import duties. There are similar sources of government revenue peculiar to each of these countries (such as the "bicycle fee" in the Cayman Islands). We will mention these, to the extent that they are relevant, as we go along.

The Bahamas. This is a very traditional, very central tax haven. Geographically, it is an archipelago. It is composed of 700 islands and uncounted rocks and reefs, stretching from Haiti on the southeast to Florida on the northwest. It has a total land area of 5,400 square miles, scattered over 70,000 square miles of ocean.

The Bahamas are usually associated in the American mind with pleasant tourism. Clearly, a country where the major means of transportation is boats sailing across vast stretches of tranquil ocean has its fascination. The pleasant climate is an extra consideration. The sun almost always shines; the temperature varies only slightly the year round, from an average minimum of seventy degrees Fahrenheit to an average maximum of eighty.

An archipelago like the Bahamas can only be organized politically and economically if there is some major island to serve as its center of trade and government. For the Bahamas, this is New Providence. It contains 50 percent of the total population (about 200,000) and the capital, Nassau.

Economically, the Bahamas thrive on tourism, the tax haven industry, and the export of petroleum products, cement, rum, salt, and ocean products. It has no heavy industry, but the export trade is a good business reason for being there.

The Bahamas are highly accessible. Nassau can be reached by air from any major airport in the United States, and it is but thirty-five minutes flight-time from Miami. There are direct flights from London, Toronto, Jamaica, Bermuda, Frankfurt, Cologne, Brussels, and Luxembourg.

Communications are no problem at all. Everyone speaks excellent English, and air mail, telegraph, direct-dial telephone, and telex services are of the highest quality.

The Bahamas are a sovereign state within the British Commonwealth, independent since 1973. Commonwealth membership means that Her Majesty the Queen is head of state, and she is locally represented by the appointed governor general. This provides a measure of safety because the governors general have traditionally been very conservative. The legislature is bicameral, the upper house appointed by the governor general on the approval, recommendation, and joint agreement of the prime minister and the leader of the opposition, and the lower house popularly elected. The upper house can delay any legislation, though eventually it must approve it. The governor general can veto any legislation he deems inconsistent with the constitution.

However, there are political snakes in the Bahamian paradise. The current government, elected right after independence, has created problems both in the granting of work permits to aliens and in exchange-control matters. Both difficulties derive from programs of "Bahamization of the economy" and "social development." However, the same government has also put into force some programs of encouragement to foreign investors and tourism, so the situation is less ominous than some rumors would have it. Moreover, the government has repeatedly promised that it will not buck the no-tax tradition.

As noted above, the legal system of the Bahamas is grounded on the English common law. This tradition is implemented by a four-level court structure: local magistrates, magistrate courts for more serious matters, a supreme court, and a court of appeals. The ultimate court of appeals is that of the whole Commonwealth, the Queen's Privy Council.

The currency and exchange control picture is not a rosy one. The local currency, the Bahamian dollar, is on par with the U.S. dollar, but it does not freely circulate with it. Exchange controls are quite strict, especially as applied to so-called resident companies, those owned by a local resident and doing business locally. These companies are only allowed to operate with local dollars and to pay foreign bills with U.S. dollars exchanged according to the official rate, each time with an express Exchange Control permission. This can be an important consideration if a local shareholder-owner (proxy) is needed to set up a tax haven company.

There are ways to avoid this difficulty. One is the formation of a nonresident company funded by a non-Bahamian company headquartered in another haven. Another arrangement is to get a general approval from Exchange Control to convert freely between local and foreign currencies on the basis of evidence that the nature of the company requires such freedom to do business effectively. Such a license for a resident corporation involves an extra obligation: an annual report to Exchange Control on the company's foreign accounts and transactions.

Only a nonresident company owned by a nonresident and operating exclusively outside the Bahamas can do business with complete freedom of exchange between currencies. This exchange control problem, coupled with difficulties that may be faced in getting a work permit for any non-Bahamian worker one might wish to employ may be reason enough for some investors to look elsewhere for a haven. Still, there are 13,000 corporations registered in the Bahamas, which indicates that, while they have become slightly less attractive as a haven, they still have their advantages.

Let us concentrate on these advantages. Whatever professional services one might need—law firms, accountants, banks, finance companies, investment advisors, stockbrokers—are available in abundance. They are of an internationally high quality, too, based on a longstanding and thriving tax haven industry. Privacy of banking arrangements in the Bahamas now easily rivals or bests that of Switzerland. There are no deals with U.S. authorities (such as the recent U.S.–Swiss agreement) that give the IRS special privileges and advantages when it comes to snooping into bank records. Nothing short of conclusive proof of a person's established leadership in the Mafia would do. Another advantage of a Bahamas bank account is that one's heirs can draw money from it without any local estate, probate, death, or inheritance duties, and without any special procedures.

As for the tax laws, there are no personal income taxes, no corporate taxes, no profit taxes, no capital gains taxes, no estate or other death taxes. On the island of New Providence there is a tax on the value of improved land. A more serious qualification is the tax on local gambling casinoes. After all, the government must get its share of this lucrative element of the tourist industry!

In accord with the general no-tax situation, there is no withholding tax of any kind. If one is a worrier, he can even incorporate in the Freeport area and get a thirty-five-year warranty against the imposition of any future tax, should one be imposed. The Bahamas are one among many tax havens that have such no-tax warranties. It is hard to say what the value of these is, if any, because a future government taking the extremely unlikely revolutionary course of introducing taxation may well refuse to respect such promises of preceding governments. Still, it is a nice touch.

The lack of any significant taxes in the Bahamas does not mean that anyone incorporating there will get off scot free. After all, the local government does deserve something in return for providing a tax haven. Whatever one pays, however, will bear no relation to his profits. There will be stamp duties on the documents of corporate registration and an annual business-license fee. The rates are quite competitive with other tax havens.

What kind of business entities can one form in the Bahamas? How? At what cost?

There are two basic types of corporations: companies limited by shares, and companies limited by guarantee. Both types belong to the general kind of corporate entities discussed in part one, but there are certain differences. Companies limited by shares have a fixed, unmodifiable authorized capital. They cannot buy back their own stock. However, a shareholder's liability is limited to his stock. If the stock is fully paid-up and the company goes bankrupt, creditors have no recourse to any of the shareholders' personal assets.

Companies limited by guarantee can reduce their share capital by buying back their shares and canceling them. This means that they can present their creditors with an unpredictable security situation. The security for bonds, debentures, and other loans is, of course, the total authorized and real capital of the corporation. If it can be reduced after bonds have been issued or loans taken out, this means that the company is legally entitled to reduce the initial assets against which it took out loans. To protect debtors in such an instance, shareholders' personal guarantees for some extra sum beyond their own investment is legally introduced.

Offshore funds, with their typically expanding-contracting capital, are therefore incorporated in the Bahamas as companies limited by guarantee. Anyone who decides to participate in the tax haven industry through an offshore fund based in the Bahamas should read the "fine print" very carefully.

Incorporating in the Bahamas requires the services of a local lawyer, who will prepare and file a memorandum of association and articles of association. Both documents are standard, and the first includes the name of the company, the address of its local registered office, its general purpose and objects, a declaration that it has limited liability of the relevant sort, and the company's capitalization (total authorized capital, the number and kind of shares, etc.). The articles of association specify the number of corporate directors and regulations concerning annual directors' meetings. On the latter point, the directors can meet anywhere, not necessarily in the Bahamas. "Alternative directors" can stand in for the regular directors, and a circular, agreed to and signed by a majority of the directors, can have the same official standing as any decisions reached by a majority at a regular directors' meeting.

The local law firm handling incorporation will charge certain fees: the charges for preparing documentation; the costs of providing five local nominee shareholders (who will sign a "deed of trust" turning over their shares to a principal after incorporation); the costs of maintaining (according to longstanding, though unwritten, tradition) a local nominee director; and the cost of "office representation" in the Bahamas (a sign displaying the company name must be posted on the building in which the registered office is located). In addition, there are these statutory requirements that must be met: a register of directors, a register of shareholders, and a minute book must be maintained in the local office, and an annual return must be submitted to the Registrar of Companies, specifying shareholders, directors, officers, the address of the registered office, and amount of share capital.

As against government fees, which are fixed, there is some variation in the fees for the above services. On the average, initial incorporation costs run about $1,500. Of course, one can shop for the least expensive services and do a bit better.

The Bahamas common law tradition also provides for trusts, which can be arranged through local trust companies. No government fees are involved because a trust is a privately constituted entity that derives its existence from a trust deed and a trust fund, not from government registration. The local trust law allows a "Cuba clause," which means that if, by some strange course of events, the Bahamas becomes a "people's democracy," the trust would automatically revert to some other country where there is a "stand-by" trustee. The use of such a clause, of course, requires that the trust assets be outside the Bahamas.

Bermuda. Bermuda is similar to the Bahamas in many respects. Like the Bahamas, it is made up of islands, seven main ones, connected by bridges, and many small coral formations, accessible from the main ones by boat. It is situated about 600 miles east of Cape Hatteras, North Carolina, and so, like the Bahamas, it is close to the East Coast. Its land area, however, is much smaller, a mere 20.5 square miles, of which two are occupied by U.S. military bases. The remaining area is densely populated by 55,000 people. Understandably, land purchases in Bermuda are difficult, both legally and financially. This is reflected in office rentals and so on.

Bermuda is a tourist's delight. It has a very moderate climate and is warmed by the Gulf Stream. Its area is hilly, with beautiful banks of flowers and lovely rainbow-hued houses.

It is highly accessible. Daily flights connect it with any major city in the world; it is but two hours from New York. It is located at the crossroads of the shipping lanes between the United States, Canada, North Europe, South America, and Oceania. Direct-dial telephone, cable, telex, and airmail services are excellent.

There are few political differences between Bermuda and the Bahamas. Bermuda is a self-governing crown colony and so is not a fully independent Commonwealth member. Like the Bahamas, it has a governor general, appointed by the Queen. This illustrious official has larger responsibilities than his Bahamian counterpart. He handles foreign relations (in accordance with British policy), security, and police. All other affairs are monitored by the democratic institutions of the colony.

The legislature is bicameral, with an appointed upper house (the Legislative Council) and an elected lower house (the House of Assembly). The governor general heads the cabinet (the Executive Council). Despite foreign affairs and defense relations with Great Britain, there exist no governmental financial relations between the colony and the mother country. All Bermudan officials, including the governor general, are paid out of local government revenues, and Great Britain gets no tax money from Bermuda. Thus, the high British taxes have no bearing on the tax situation in Bermuda. The self-governing nature of Bermuda means that any changes in the tax laws or other legislation cannot be imposed from without; they can only emerge from the local legislature.

The legal tradition in Bermuda derives from ancient, pre–1612, British common law, modified by locally generated common law. The legal framework is three-tiered: magistrate courts, a supreme court, and a court of appeals. As in all Commonwealth countries, the ultimate court of appeals is the Queen's Privy Council in London.

The local currency, the Bermudan dollar, is on par with the U.S. dollar. As in the Bahamas, there are exchange controls on residents and resident companies.

Bermuda is similar to the Bahamas in having a large range of high quality professional services available. Very strict banking legislation has resulted in there being only four banks, which, by law, are locally controlled; local stock ownership, combined, cannot legally fall below 60 percent.

The British tradition in Bermuda means that there are strong ties between accountants, lawyers, trust companies, and banks. Once one chooses his accountant, say, this gentleman will "strongly recommend" the lawyer, trust company, and bank to be used, stressing that he is "accustomed" to working with them. This may seem a bit restrictive, but it guarantees good cooperation between firms that otherwise might not cooperate in one's best interests.

As in the Bahamas, local bank deposits have certain attractive features; the depositer can choose the currency, there is no withholding or other tax on interest, and he can have a joint account with his spouse allowing that he or she is to have immediate title to the assets in case of the other's death. If, though, both account holders die at the same time, any heirs will have access to the account only by reference to a properly executed will approved by a court, and the will will be a matter of public record.

As for taxes, there is no personal income tax, no

corporation tax, no profits tax, no capital tax, no capital gains tax, no withholding tax, no inheritance tax. There are import duties and a 10 percent property levy on the rental value of houses and land. To take advantage of this happy situation, one can either incorporate or form a local trust.

Incorporation in Bermuda was made simpler in August 1970. Previously, any incorporation required a special private legislative act. To incorporate one had to offer a petition to the local parliament through a legal representative. The legislature would then vote on the proposal and, eventually, approve it. This superceremonious method of incorporation still exists and must be used if any aspect of the structure, internal organization, or mode of operation of an intended company deviates from the pattern dictated by the General Corporation Law enacted in August 1970. However, if the corporation is a "normal" one, incorporation can be accomplished without such legislative ceremonies by submitting the standard type of documents for the Registrar of Companies to approve.

There are two basic types of companies recognized by Bermudan corporate legislation, local companies and exempt companies. Local companies are those formed by Bermudans for purposes of internal trade or Bermuda-based international trade (import to and export from Bermuda). Such companies have a minimum percentage of local stock ownership, prescribed by law, are subject to strict exchange control, and have no guaranteed immunity against future taxes.

An exempt company is free of the first two restrictions above, and is given an official guarantee against the levying of future taxes for thirty years. However, an exempt company is restricted as follows: (1) It cannot buy, lease, or sell land, mortgages secured by land, or bonds and debentures secured by land without special permission. (2) It cannot buy shares of local companies. (3) It cannot locally sell whatever it produces without special ad hoc permission. These limitations narrow "business justification" possibilities for Bermudan incorporation, to say the least, and there is no way around them.

Incorporation in Bermuda is more difficult than in the Bahamas. The official costs are: a stamp duty of 25 percent on the shares of the company's authorized capital (the use of nominee shareholders involves an extra duty of 50 percent of the value of the shares); $480 for exempt status, paid on incorporation and annually thereafter; a stamp duty of 0.2 percent on bonds and debentures issued; and a $560 annual fee for an "ordinary" company and a $1,000 annual fee for a finance, insurance, or mutual fund company.

In addition to the financial burdens, there is a "screening" of incorporation applications. A committee chaired by a member of Parliament examines bank references to eliminate Mafia types and such. This screening slows things up, and may take a month.

Taking into account the various professional services that are needed for incorporation as well as the high government fees, both incorporation and annual maintenance run to $2,000–$2,500 a year depending on the specific services required.

Bermudan trusts are much less costly. A stamp duty of 0.25 percent of the initial fund (plus the same percentage on any later increase in the fund) is the total governmental cost. A trust is not locally taxed on its profits, but if its beneficiaries are aliens, it cannot, in view of the land scarcity, invest in local real estate without special approval from the Executive Council—which turns a deaf ear to all such requests.

Even if the disadvantages noted above do not discourage a potential investor, the Bermudan political and social situation may. There is a policy of "Bermudization." There are problems with immigration and work permits for aliens; hiring a local office is difficult in view of the land restrictions; the distinction between local and alien companies is very strict. There has already been an attempt, defeated in Parliament, to introduce an income tax. Local companies pay a 5 percent "payroll tax," which means that on each $100 an employee gets, the company has to pay the government an extra $5. This does not apply as yet to exempt companies, and they are, moreover, guaranteed against it. But this is a bad sign for a tax haven. (Remember, the U.S. income tax started at 5 percent.) There is also some racial tension between whites and blacks (60 percent of the population is black). The murder of the governor general, his aide, and the chief of police in 1973 may have been political, though it probably was not.

Thus, given a choice between Bermuda and the Bahamas, the Bahamas may make the better bet. The only advantage Bermuda seems to have is the extra respectability conferred on Bermudan companies by the screening process.

The Cayman Islands. To assert that the Cayman Islands are superior to both the Bahamas and Bermuda as a tax haven is to assert an opinion. To point out that many tax haven companies, established firmly for many years in the Bahamas and Bermuda, have recently transferred their bases of operation to the Caymans is to point out a fact, a fact worth paying attention to.

Like Bermuda and the Bahamas, the Caymans are —obviously—a collection of islands. There are three of them, located 475 miles south of Miami and 200 miles north of Montego Bay. Of the three, Grand Cayman, as its name implies, is the major one; it is there that both the capital and most business activities are located. Its area is significantly greater than that of the other two, seventy-six square miles, as against Cayman Brace's fourteen and Little Cayman's ten. Cayman Brace is east of Grand Cayman, and Little Cayman lies between the two larger islands.

This trio is rather hot. The only factor differentiating the tropical nature of the Caymans from West Africa is the trade winds, which cool them off—a little.

The Caymans are about five times larger than Bermuda, and they are much less densely populated, with 12,000 people, 1,500 of whom are seamen who are rarely home. Thus, the Bermudan "land sensitivity" reflected in harsh strictures on land purchases by foreigners and in high real estate costs has a very moderate counterpart in the Caymans.

Being a tax haven is for the Caymans, like Bermuda and the Bahamas, a tradition based on British rule. Here, however, the tradition is bolstered by a legend. In 1798 the islanders heroically saved from tragic death at sea a British royal prince and his mentor, an admiral, and King George III gratefully granted the islanders eternal tax exemption. Scholars may concern themselves with the authenticity of the legend, and its legal significance at present is dubious. But it is very significant as a predictor of the future; such a strong tax haven tradition would make it very difficult to introduce any sort of taxation.

Not that there is any special reason to worry about the Caymans, as there may be with Bermuda and the Bahamas. The latter two are not, from the point of view of governmental economic and foreign policy, enthusiastically dedicated to being havens. They became so only as a by-product of their total no-tax tradition. The Cayman Islands government, on the other hand, is very keen on the tax haven industry, a major factor in local economic growth. Thus, the consideration of expected future stability favors the Caymans. It is important to see, therefore, whether they are inferior to their competition in other respects.

One can fly to the Caymans from Miami, Kingston, Jamaica, and Costa Rica. Only three airlines serve the islands at this time: Southern Airways, Cayman Islands Airways, and LASCSA. But work is under way on the airport to improve its facilities, and two additional airline companies have indicated readiness to begin service when this is completed. Communications are slightly inferior to those in the Bahamas and Bermuda. There are adequate airmail, telephone, telex, and cable services.

Politically, the Caymans are a crown colony by

choice. In 1962, when Jamaica became independent of Great Britain and the Caymans were a dependency of Jamaica, the Caymans decided by national referendum against independence or a Jamaican connection and for the status of a crown colony. This indicates a rather unusual traditional conservatism in this era of "national independence" and the "fight against colonialistic imperialism," and it is a strong predictor of stability.

The local population is racially mixed, but mixed in the right way. There is a minority of pure Europeans (20 percent) and pure Africans (20 percent) and a racially mixed majority (60 percent). This indicates that racial tension, prejudice, segregation, and such, were never serious factors in the Caymans and are likely to become even less so. This, again, is important because leftist governments often come to power employing racial strife as a major crutch. Here leftists would not have much to lean on.

The government is headed by a governor general, an appointee of the Queen. He heads the Executive Council, his cabinet. The council members are partially elected, partially appointed by the governor general. There is a one-house legislature, the Legislative Assembly, elected by universal suffrage. Recent elections and day-to-day political life do not indicate any basic left-right polarization. The Caymans are a politically quiet place.

The law is British common law modified by local legislation. The court structure is similar to those of Bermuda and the Bahamas. Corporate legislation is modernized and efficient. Exchange controls are somewhat less strict than in Bermuda and the Bahamas. They involve major restrictions on local residents, but a "nonresident" company dealing outside the islands can be formed, eliminating all exchange-control considerations. The only restriction on such a company is that it cannot use the local currency.

The Caymans' superiority over the Bahamas and Bermuda is not modified by a comparison of available professional services. A broad range of high quality legal, banking, accounting, finance, and trust services is available. There are seven large banks, and there is a traditional association between banks and trust companies.

The Caymans' tax structure is superior to those of Bermuda and the Bahamas. The *only* sources of government revenue are stamp and import duties. An automatic no-tax guarantee of twenty years is granted to nonresident exempted corporations, and there is a fifty-year guarantee to trusts. There is virtually no tax department.

Incorporation is quicker, easier, and cheaper than in the Bahamas and Bermuda. A memorandum of association, involving three initial shareholders (which a legal representative can supply as proxies), is required. It has to specify the usual details: name of corporation, address of its local registered office, statement of purposes, statement that it has limited liability, and its capitalization (amount of authorized capital, division into shares, and par value of shares). On payment of a $180 registration fee, the Registrar of Companies issues an immediate certificate of incorporation and files the memorandum. There is no Bermuda-type investigation of bank references. Maintenance of a corporation is quite reasonable. An annual $40 fee is required, as are the standard office services, supplied by an agent for a modest fee. This same agent will also submit the required annual return to the government. This has nothing to do with finances. It merely specifies the name of the company, the address of the local registered office, the authorized capital, the issued capital (total par value of issued stock), and the names and addresses of the *nominal* shareholders. This annual return has to be accompanied by the $40 annual fee.

Total costs of incorporation run about $1,000—the only constant being the government fee, while the agent's fees vary. Annual maintenance averages about $650.

All of the above applies to an "ordinary" company. There are also exempt companies. The above-mentioned twenty-year no-tax guarantee applies only to them. The fact that a company operates in trade outside the Caymans does not mean it has to be exempt. It is up to the incorporators to consider the relative advantages and disadvantages. An exempt company, apart from the twenty-year guarantee, can omit from its name the "Ltd." required of other companies, can issue shares without par value, can dispense with the formality of annual shareholder meetings, and can keep private, with no representation in any official records, the names of shareholders.

Of course, all these benefits cost. The registration fee is between $750 and $1,600 depending on a company's authorized capital. The first figure applies up to $400,000, and there is an increase of 0.1 percent on any additional authorized capital. The annual fee is also larger, from a minimum of $200 to a maximum of $1,000 (based on 0.05 percent of the authorized capital of a company). Legal costs and annual maintenance run about 50 percent higher too. Even with these fees, a Caymans exempt company costs about the same as a Bermudan nonresident company, and apart from the above advantages, it can also issue bearer shares, and there is no extra charge in the form of stamp duties on the transfer of shares.

Another advantage of an exempt company is the possibility of redeemable preference shares, which at the time of liquidation have priority over ordinary shares in being paid up by the company to the shareholder but which usually have no voting power. Such shares can be useful if one wants to finance his corporation not by taking out loans but by issuing new stock without at the same time compromising control of the company.

The reader may have wondered why articles of association were not mentioned above. The reason is that in the Caymans there is a "Table A" that substitutes for these uniformly in a manner that creates only minor inconvenience. This table is not a curse of uniformity but a blessing of not worrying over what are usually irrelevant formalities. One can at any time offer articles of association, modifying Table A as he wishes, leaving the table to apply automatically to matters not mentioned in the modification. The table is thus a legal convention created to enhance convenience of local incorporation.

Of course, the common law tradition of the Caymans allows not only corporations but trusts. Trust companies galore compete to be of service.

The trust deed requires a stamp duty and a nominal fee for official recording. However, total formation costs with an average trust company are only about $300. There are no undue limitations concerning either trust founders or beneficiaries, and, of course, no taxes on trust profits, which can accumulate and multiply nicely, enriched by whatever extra additions to its principal one may care to make. For an extra expense of $300 ($200 to the government for registration), one can get the trust counterpart of an exempt corporation, the exempt trust. It has a fifty-year guarantee against future taxes, but its annual maintenance cost includes a yearly $120 government fee. As against the exempt corporation, which offers a package of business advantages apart from the no-tax warranty, the exempt trust is worthwhile only for the real worrying types, who seriously believe that in the Caymans any form of tax on incomes of trusts with foreign founders, trustees, and, possibly, assets will be introduced.

As we have already indicated, the Bahamas are a haven for banks. Comparably, the Caymans are a real bonanza. An "offshore" bank license (for a bank with no local business) costs a mere $4,200, while an insurance company license costs no more than an "ordinary" company. As against the heavy burden of regulations on banks and insurance companies in the United States, or even Bermuda, there is very light regulation in the Caymans. This, of course, means that the overseas credibility of a Caymans bank or insurance company depends on its reputation. A Caymans bank is a truly free-market institution. It is trusted by depositors and creditors to the extent that it has established by sound practices that it is trustworthy.

The Caymans offer a large range of possible business activities. Moreover, work permits and immigration licenses are easy to obtain for whatever foreign personnel a company might want to bring in. There is virtually no nationalistic spirit or land-scarcity anxiety, and bank privacy is strongly guarded. A government official who breaches bank privacy can expect heavy fines and a prison term.

Clearly, the Caymans are superior in virtually every respect—future no-tax security, costs, expediency of incorporation, flexibility of corporate structure, business opportunities, privacy, immigration, and prospects for land ownership. The very positive government interest in the tax haven industry is also a big plus. While there is one other no-tax haven, the New Hebrides, which is in some ways superior to the traditional havens of the Bahamas and Bermuda, it cannot compete with the Cayman Islands. Whatever the specific circumstances, the Caymans are tops, as the transfer there of many firms from the Bahamas and Bermuda confirms. Moving a corporate base of operations is costly, and it is not done unless the considerations in favor of the move substantially outweigh the costs.

The New Hebrides. Like the Bahamas, Bermuda, and the Caymans, the New Hebrides are an island archipelago, but they are a bit more isolated. The nearest population center of any significance is Sydney, Australia, 1,200 miles to the south. The New Hebrides are made up of an almost uncountable collection of islands, islets, atolls, and coral reefs, scattered across a vast stretch of the South Pacific.

The huge distances involved, both between the U.S. and the New Hebrides and between the islands themselves, make for significant communications problems. The New Hebrides can be reached by air from Brisbane, Australia, the Fijis, or Noumea, New Caledonia, but there are no direct flights from the United States. Needless to say, this means that getting there requires a large expenditure of time and money. While telephone, telex, cable, and airmail services exist, they leave much to be desired. For example, an office building may have but one telephone booth shared by all its tenants. Airmail involves no fewer than two "connecting" flights, a minimum of seventeen hours in the air, and who knows how many hours waiting time on the ground. Telex is through Paris, of all places, and as for cable, well, one should not complain too much.

Moreover, the New Hebrides are on the "wrong" side of the planet, being located in the Southern Hemisphere, where people walk around with their heads down and their heels in the air, or, to be less flippant, sleep when Americans are awake and vice versa. This, together with the technical communications difficulties, makes it more than a bit hard to run, say, a stock-exchange business in the islands. However, the exotic locale of the New Hebrides and their bizarre social and political structures make them attractive to tourists and other odd sorts. Tourism, beef export, and the tax haven industry are the major economic activities.

Now, what do I mean by "bizarre social and political structures"? To begin with, the population consists of 80,000 native Melanesians and 10,000

Europeans, who do not mix. Moreover, the Europeans are segregated into two communities, French and English, each living according to the traditions of its homeland. These communities keep aloof from each other, not involving themselves in any cross-national trade, business, or cultural enterprise. This racial and cultural segregation is surprisingly combined with very peaceful relations. The separation is more a matter of indifference than hostility.

The peculiar social structure results in a no less peculiar political structure. There are three governments coexisting in a very strange relationship. There is a British commissioner, whose authority extends to all English-origin residents and any newcomer Europeans electing to be part of the British legal community. There is a French commissioner, governing the French locals and any newcomers who opt for French law. There is the native tribal system, completely independent of the British and French.

Recently, the natives (or, rather, some of them) have created a federation of some of the islands, which they call Nagri Gramel. Nagri Gramel declared independence of colonial rule and established a parliamentary democracy based on a constitution that would warm the heart of any cussed individualist: taxes are unconstitutional, individual rights to life, liberty, and property are guaranteed, and so on. This new government, however, has not gained the support of all the natives, and it is all but ignored by world governments, including the local British and French commissioners. This is an odd situation, for while the new native government could be considered a "revolutionary independent" outfit, the fact that the British and French (and most of the natives) simply ignore it rather than resisting or supporting it, puts it in a strange limbo. The British and French have never tried to extend their authority to the native population, who have technically been stateless. Consequently, the natives themselves are largely indifferent to the new "government." In any event, Nagri Gramel is of no help to anyone seeking to establish a tax haven corporation or trust because of its lack of international recognition.

The British-French arrangement is based on a codominium agreement reached by Great Britain and France in 1911. The agreement simply divides rule, and the only kind of cooperation is in legal matters. While each community abides by its own code of law and employs its own court system, there is a "common" court of appeals. The chairman of this court of appeals is supposed to be appointed by the king of Spain! Since the recently enthroned Spanish king, Juan Carlos, has ignored this responsibility (he does have a few other matters to worry about), the current chairman was selected by the long-standing practice of alternating British and French chairmen. Unsurprisingly, this arrangement involves a fifty-fifty split of the chairman's salary.

One of the major advantages of the New Hebrides is that there is no legislature of any sort. English is the official language for the British, as is French for the French. The natives have some 110 different languages of their own.

Another advantage following from this rampant pluralism that makes the New Hebrides superior to the three other no-tax havens considered here is that there are two official currencies, the French franc for the French, the Australian dollar for the British. Clearly, no exchange control could operate effectively under such circumstances, so there is none.

There are no taxes in either the French or the English community. However, only the British setup will be considered here, both because of the common law tradition and because the French have no tax haven industry. (Instead they speculate in land.) On the British side the tax haven industry has given rise to a large number of professional services: eight banks, seven accountancy firms, six law firms, and six trust firms, all of high quality.

The two governments finance themselves through export-import duties, license fees for local trade, land registration fees and land taxes imposed when land is subdivided. There are also stamp duties, company and bank registration fees, and ship registration fees on the British side.

The reader may well be wondering what might be the redeeming advantage of incorporating in the New Hebrides. There is one: absolute privacy. An exempt company, incorporated by foreigners for the purpose of foreign trade, is fully defended against any disclosure of information to anyone, whether foreign government or private snooper. A government official who reveals information about a company faces heavy penalties.

Incorporation in the New Hebrides involves a prescreening process, although it is done differently than in Bermuda. It is the responsibility of the incorporator's local representative trust company. References (banks, etc.) are required. When incorporation goes through (the documentation and corporate structure is standard, and the costs are about $1,000 Australian, for incorporation and for annual maintenance) the law requires a local director from the trust company. He is not merely a nominee. The local director supervises company activities closely. If he finds out that the incorporator has Mafia connections or what have you, he will resign and inform the government, which will then deregister the company.

An unfortunate requirement is that for a local annual directors' meeting. This does not mean that the real directors have to fly all the way to the New Hebrides, but even if this requirement is met by a pro forma gathering of proxies, the need for "alternate directors" on the company payroll keeps annual maintenance costs rather high.

Trusts can be established in the New Hebrides in the usual fashion. The local common law tradition is almost purely British. The only local modifications derive from court precedents over the last seventy years or so.

Comparing the New Hebrides and the Caymans, the Caymans obviously come out on top in virtually every important respect. Privacy is legally stricter in the New Hebrides, but it is combined with greater government intervention through the supervisory local director and the screening process. The only advantage of the New Hebrides is the complete absence of exchange controls, unless one has a penchant for Gauguin-like isolation.

EIGHT

Foreign-Source-Income Havens: Profits Abroad—Tax Free

It is perhaps easier for an American reader to understand no-tax havens than those that tax only locally earned income. Bermuda, the Bahamas, the Caymans, and the New Hebrides provide natural and obvious no-tax alternatives to the American tax system. The United States taxes all of income, regardless of its sources. The no-tax havens tax none of it.

There is a third possibility, countries that tax only income generated locally—at rates far lower than those imposed by Uncle Sam. If one lives and works in one of these places, the income from his work is taxed. However, if he lives there and derives income from abroad, or if he does not personally reside there but his legal "shadow" (a corporation or trust) does, then that foreign income is not locally taxable.

This illustrates an important distinction in taxing practices. Tax systems can be compared not only in terms of the types of taxes they impose, the proportions, or rates, they use to determine the amount of tax due, but also in terms of the sources of income that are considered taxable.

Countries that impose no taxes on foreign income are not always tax havens. Most Latin American countries tax only local income, but most of them are too politically and economically unstable to be worth even a passing thought. Moreover, governments that exclude foreign-source income from taxation are unlikely to face much political opposition if they decide to tax such income. The populations of such specialized havens are used to taxes. In other words, if there is any guarantee of the continuation of the practice of exempting foreign income from taxation, it lies in a sustained desire of governments to earn revenues from the tax haven industry in other ways. Unfortunately, such policies tend to be as fragile as the governments taking advantage of them. While the continuation of current policy can be reasonably expected in most no-tax havens because of the strong influence of tradition and simple individual self-interest. No such automatic projection of stability can be made in most no-tax-on-foreign-source-income countries.

But there are some exceptions. Each of them merits attention because all offer the possibility of creating a local company, the bulk of whose investment is abroad and thus free from local taxation, but that is located in a country that does not possess a tax haven reputation. To be more specific, if one has a Hong Kong corporation, he may very well have some very good business (as opposed to tax) motivation for it: cheap local labor, excellent possibilities for international trade, etc. A Bermudan exempt company, however, instantly suggests tax avoidance to a suspicious mind.

Another general advantage of these havens is that their governments usually want foreign investment. In some of these countries, foreign investors get preferential treatment that may mean not only tax advantages, but subsidies, marketing privileges, etc. So let us look at these unusual lands.

Panama. Panama deserves first mention here because it is already so widely used by American individuals and corporations as a base for their foreign operations. It is notable for the combination of tax and business advantages it offers.

A major reason for the popularity of Panama is its location. It is the link between North and South America, and it includes the famous Panama Canal, connecting the Atlantic and the Pacific. Its total land area is 29,700 square miles, containing a population of about 1.5 million. The majority of these people (60 percent) live off the land. The capital, Panama City, contains most of the urbanized population (500,000 residents), and most of the rest live in the other major city, Colon. Colon's significance, economically, derives from its freeport facilities, which we will discuss later.

A visitor to Panama is in no danger of freezing. The climate is tropical—hot, with heavy rains (50 inches a year on the Pacific side, 150 on the Atlantic. There is a dry season from mid-December through the end of April.

One can reach Panama more easily than virtually any other tax haven. It is even possible to drive there! Just take the Inter-American Highway. To save time, a plane from most any of the major cities of the United States will put a visitor down at the airport at Tocumento, fourteen miles from Panama City. Some nineteen airlines serve Panama. If sea travel is preferred, Panama has four excellent ports: Cristobal, at the Atlantic end of the Canal, Balboa, at the Pacific end, and Puerto Armuelles and Bahias de las Rouge. Traveling by car may take less time than going by ship, it is cheaper, and both the Inter-American Highway and the local roads are excellent.

Telecommunication is extremely efficient because Panama is an international crossroads of trade. There is direct telephone service via satellite and very reliable telex, cable, and airmail.

Politically, Panama is a "banana republic." It has, on the surface, a democratic election system that every six years is supposed to produce a turnover in the unicameral legislature, the National Assembly, while the "chief of state," the president, and the vice president are supposed to be elected by the assembly. The chief of state is the chairman of the national cabinet and roughly corresponds to the prime minister in a parliamentary government. On paper, the National Assembly has the job of examining and approving or disapproving legislation drafted by a national legislative commission. In reality, Panama is a typical Latin American dictatorship run by whoever happens to be in charge of the National Guard (army), with all the republican and democratic trappings as mere windowdressing. However, the military leaders—even the leftists—never seem to tinker with the tax and corporation laws. There is a kind of economic freedom absolutely unaffected by political turnover. The rulers seem to have the good sense not to slay the goose that lays the golden eggs.

Another indication of the considerable independence and stability of economic policy is the structure of the Panamanian civil service and government. We are used to a public bureaucracy in which each department is headed by a political appointee to a ministerial/secretarial position. In Panama a variety of governmental functions are handled by purely bureaucratic agencies with no political honchos. Electricity and hydraulic resources, national telecommunications, tourism, social security, all these functions are handled by a semiautonomous official institute, which is not under any cabinet minister.

Spanish is the official language, but English is very widely used because of the influence of the Canal Zone. Most professionals and businessmen speak English. Thus, there is virtually no language barrier.

A very pleasing feature of Panama is the absolute monetary freedom. The local Balboa is on par with the U.S. dollar and exchanges freely with it. All paper money is American. The lack of exchange controls implies that the government cannot regulate the money supply, and there is no central bank. This means that inflation and government-produced depression are unlikely. Add to this banking legislation comparable to that of the Switzerland of old: numbered accounts in the currency the account holder designates and very strictly enforced secrecy laws.

The central position of Panama in inter-American

as well as transoceanic trade means that its professional services—banking, accountancy, legal, brokerage—are of the highest quality and intensely competitive. There are sixty banks, both local and international, and more are springing up monthly. Name any major international banking organization and it has a branch in Panama.

There are many Panamanian management companies that can handle local corporate creation and management in all necessary aspects. They play a role analogous to that of Bahamian and other trust companies, and they even offer trust services. (However, in view of the fact that Panama is a civil law country, trusts, though legally possible, are best avoided.) They will handle anything and everything: incorporation, registration of assets, provision of all required nominee officers and directors to cover the various requirements of corporation law, etc. They will even conduct feasibility studies on the advisability of alternative possible investments.

Panama taxes locally generated income and exempts from tax all income generated abroad. This policy has existed since the country was founded in 1903, good reason to believe that the policy is too well entrenched to be changed with ease. The income tax on the local income of residents is progressive; brackets range from 2 percent on the first $1,000 to 46 percent on any income above $200,000. This is better than U.S. rates, but still heavy. If one is in the country less than six months in a year and generates local income, he is not exempted from tax altogether or even allowed to "spread" his income over the whole year. Rather, he pays taxes on a pro rata basis; the ratio of Panamanian residence duration to a full year is the basis for calculation. Thus, Panama is not ideal for an immigrant tax-refugee. (A curious feature of local tax laws is that tax evasion creates liability for fines but not for a prison term.)

On the bright side, all income generated by movement of commodities that never pass through Panama (even though they may be invoiced in Panama and managed from a Panamanian office) is completely excempt from taxation. Thus, there are good business reasons—"business motivation"—for setting up a Panama-based corporation. Moreover, if dividends are paid to stockholders residing outside Panama, no withholding tax applies, provided the profit underlying the dividends is all derived from sources external to Panama. Similarly, if one inherits property owned by a Panamanian corporation (by inheriting the stock) and the assets themselves are outside Panama, no inheritance taxes apply.

Even if the assets are in Panama, inheritance taxation is quite liberal when compared to the United States. Inheritance taxes are calculated after the estate is divided between the various heirs. The first $30,000 is exempt from tax (this means that if an estate of $150,000 were divided equally among five heirs, each would inherit $30,000 tax-free); close relatives are taxed much less than more distant relatives; and tax rates are only 80 percent of their officially stated ratio because of an automatic 20 percent deduction of tax liability.

The fact that overseas operations based in Panama are not taxed, together with easily demonstrated business motivation for Panamanian operations, the free exchange of currencies, and the economically strategic position of the country account for the 35,000 corporations, mostly foreign, that are registered in Panama—more than in any other tax haven. This large corporate presence is, in itself, the strongest guarantee of future preservation of the tax-free-foreign-income policy. Any change of this policy would scare off most of the 35,000 companies, terminate the flow of money they feed into the Panamanian economy and the government treasury, and thus would be a vast net loss. The free market situation in the international tax haven industry, following from the existence of many alternative havens all competing for patronage, should keep Panama very much "in line."

Panama's principal claim to fame as a haven for foreign companies is based on the shipping industry. Like Liberia, Panama offers special advantages for shipowners who elect to fly its flag as a "flag of convenience." The cost of ship registration in Panama is only one dollar per ton plus a bill of sale registration fee of twenty cents per ton (net). The annual tax after registration is a mere ten cents per ton. Even if a shipping company regularly imports and exports from and to Panama, none of its income or profits (or the salaries of its crews, for that matter) are subject to any Panamanian tax. Moreover, Panama's maritime labor regulations are much more liberal than those of the United States, so most U.S. shipping companies that operate internationally register in Panama. The United States has officially recognized this state of affairs for defense reasons. A special agreement between the United States and Panama allows Panama registered ships owned by

U.S. residents and corporations to support U.S. armed forces in time of war.

Let us now review Panamanian corporate law. Fortunately, it is based on the Delaware laws of 1927 (without amendments). As the reader may know, Delaware is the best U.S. state in which to incorporate because of its very advantageous corporation laws. In Panama incorporation requires two incorporators, who must execute the articles of incorporation before the Panamanian counterpart of a notary public. These two are usually nominees, employees of a local management company. The articles of incorporation are recorded at the public registry office, and the later costs of maintenance can be reduced to a $100 annual fee to a local legal representative. Nominee "incorporators," though nominally shareholders at the time of incorporation, will sign a deed of transfer returning their stock to their principal(s) after incorporation has been effected.

The articles of incorporation must include the usual details: (1) company name, with the standard designation for a corporate entity, (2) a statement, however general, of the objects of the corporation, (3) capitalization, specifying both the total amount of authorized capital (which determines the limit of the company's liabilities) and its division into shares with their respective par values (shares with no par value can be issued, but then the government assumes that each share has the nominal par value of $20 for the purpose of computing the registration tax), (4) specification of the nature of the shares— registered or bearer, common or preferred, voting or nonvoting, (5) names and addresses of at least three directors (usually nominees hired for an annual fee), (6) names and addresses of officers (again, nominees—who can be the same individuals serving as directors), (7) the duration of the corporation, which can be a specified limited period or "forever," (8) name and address of the local legal representative of the company, and (9) the domicile of the corporation (e.g., Panama City, Panama).

How costly is incorporation? Here is a breakdown of average usual expenses:

Notary (including stamp duty)	$100
Capital stock tax	20
Public registry fee and expenses	20
Legal fees and expenses	350
Minute book and stock-register book	20
Rubrication of minute books (see below)	10
Miscellaneous	10
Total	$530

However, the cost could be higher. The capital stock tax above is computed for a legally authorized capital of $10,000. Each additional $1,000 up to $100,000 involves an extra seventy-five cents; each additional $1,000 from the first $100,000 to the first million costs fifty cents; and each additional $1,000 from $1 million on up costs an extra ten cents. Similarly, the notary fees above assume a standard charter of incorporation. If the charter is extremely complex, the cost may be higher.

Annual corporate maintenance costs very little, about $100–$200. The low fees stem from the fact that the local legal representative has only to exist;

he has no reports to file nor any other work to do.

Thus, neither incorporation nor company maintenance is very expensive in Panama. It is certainly much less expensive than the comparative action in Bermuda, the Bahamas, and even the Caymans. And one gets the same tax advantages for income generated outside the country. Moreover, there is further advantage to be enjoyed by Panamanian companies that deal exclusively outside Panama. They need keep no financial records locally, nor do they have to submit any annual financial reports with the local tax authorities. What has to be kept locally is a stock-register book for registered stock and a minute book for meetings of stockholders. The latter must be rubricated (for a special fee) by a local judge. It is also bound in such a way that the minutes must be entered manually; typed minutes cannot be filed in. This, though, is just an unimportant nuisance, not a serious consideration.

Another nuisance concerns stockholders' meetings. If not physically held in Panama, these have to be officially sanctioned by the Panamanian consul in the country where they are held and then registered in the minute book in Panama. Alternatively, they can be made official by the signature of the corporate secretary, the person whose name is recorded in the mercantile registry as the corporation's secretary. Again, this is merely a curiosity of some slight inconvenience, not a major problem.

If, however, a company does local business in Panama, it becomes subject to taxes on its locally generated income. In this case, a general ledger, a general journal, an inventory, and a balance sheet must be maintained. A commercial business license may also be needed. This could be bypassed by handling Panamanian business through a corporation domiciled in, say, the Cayman Islands. The Panamanian withholding tax is lower than the corporate income tax on locally operating companies. In any event, if a Panamanian corporation is not in any way directly involved in domestic business activities in Panama, no annual report of *any kind* has to be made. Even interest generated locally on local bank deposits is free from any local tax or withholding. Thus, for a sum of about $500 for incorporation and $100–$200 a year in maintenance costs, a company can enjoy virtually complete business privacy—no reports, no books, no anything.

Another advantage of Panama, apart from its very private corporations, the low costs of annual maintenance, and the free exchange of currencies, is the Colon Free Zone. Located at the Atlantic entrance to Panama and accessible by air and sea from every corner of the Western Hemisphere, it is very active economically, with an annual trade volume of about $950 million. At this writing, it has attracted 1,200 international companies from the United States, Japan, and Europe. Its freedom of trade involves complete exemption from duties on merchandise imported into it, packed, labelled and/or assembled in it, and reshipped from it. Moreover, no commercial licenses are needed.

How to use the freeport facilities depends on the size of the commercial operations one intends to conduct from them. Land can be leased there, and warehouse or other facilities can be built on it. The cost is fifteen cents per square meter per month. The usual lease is for twenty years and is renewable. Warehouse space can be leased too. This runs about sixty-three to seventy-five cents per square meter per month, the specific rate being determined by the amount of total leased space and the length of the lease—the larger the space and the longer the lease, the lower the fee. Finally, local warehouses are also available for fees based on the value of the total merchandise stored. Clearly, the leasing of space and construction of warehouses for hire is a lucrative business possibility in the Free Zone.

Unfortunately, the freeport, although duty-free, is not totally tax-free. Merchandise that physically passes through the Colon area and is subject to some form of local processing—repacking, labelling, etc.—is taxed by the Panamanian government. The tax rates, however, are extremely low. They are based on a 1954 income tax law, under which corporate income tax was but 30 percent on net profit. Add to this a 90 percent "tax discount" applicable in the Colon Free Zone, and the result is a negligible 3 percent tax on net profit from all merchandise that physically passes through Colon not later sold in Panama. (Standard taxes apply to all Free Zone goods resold in Panama.)

Summing up, Panama has an impressive array of advantages over its competition: (1) No exchange controls, no federal reserve or central bank, complete monetary freedom. (2) No taxes and no required financial or other annual reports by corporations doing business exclusively outside Panama. (3) Relatively low incorporation and annual maintenance costs, with a rich array of professional services to take care of everything. (4) The possibility of safeguarding privacy with both bearer shares and numbered bank accounts in the currency of the depositor's choice, with tax-free interest. (5) The possibility of dabbling in the shipping industry with minimal governmental costs, costs that are a low function of tonnage and are unrelated to profits. (6) The prospects of doing business through the Colon Free Zone, duty-free and almost tax-free. (7) A tradition of being a tax haven, bolstered by the local presence of many tax haven corporations, creating a virtual knockout argument for any future government tempted to impose taxes on foreign income. (8) The ease of supplying a business justification for a Panamanian corporation should the need arise.

Of course, Panama is not perfect. As with the no-tax havens we dealt with in chapter seven, it is not a good location for a holding company holding U.S. stock. Panama has no double-taxation agreement with any country. A Panamanian corporation that holds U.S. stock is subject to the full 30 percent U.S. withholding tax on all its U.S.-source income. However, in a multihaven arrangement of the sort already discussed, Panama could compete with a pure no-tax haven, even the Caymans.

Hong Kong. The British Crown Colony of Hong Kong is quite similar to Panama in many respects. It taxes only locally generated income. Its tax rates are extremely low by U.S. and even Panamanian standards. Its haven status is subsidiary to its role as an international business center, strategically located as "the gateway to the Orient" and as a station between the West and the vast markets of the speedily developing East.

Hong Kong also enjoys incredibly cheap labor, for it lies on the southeast coast of Communist China, bordering on the province of Kwangtung. Refugees from Communist tyranny reach it daily, and their survival requires that they work. The population of Hong Kong is extremely dense, probably the most crowded in the world. At least 4 million people live in a total area of about 400 square miles ("at least" because there are thousands of unregistered refugees). The island of Hong Kong and some smaller islands comprise about 33 square miles, and the remaining area (the New Territories) is mainland and island territory belonging to Red China. This area was leased from pre-Communist China by Great Britain. The lease is scheduled to run out on June 30, 1997.

It is an interesting matter for speculation whether the Communists might declare the lease signed by their "capitalist, imperialist, fascist" predecessors and "imperialist, colonialist pigs" invalid. An even more disturbing issue of speculation is whether the lease will be renewed. Nothing is certain, but the best guess is that Peking will let things stand as they are. The Communists need Hong Kong as a valuable source of hard currency and trade with the outside world. It is unlikely that they will rock the boat.

In any event, in this tiny area of 400 square miles live at least 4 million individuals, 95 percent of whom are Chinese. This population of 10,000 and more per square mile makes for an extremely competitive and varied labor market, and no such Western ills as unions and their like are conceivable. In other words, quite apart from tax considerations, there are very good business reasons for setting up shop in Hong Kong.

The crown colony's prominence as a trade and manufacturing center means that there are superb transportation and communications facilities. Major airlines connect Hong Kong by very frequent flights to every major city in the world. Ships are also available to anywhere, and the British civil service tradition, coupled with the pressures of demand, makes its airmail, telex, and international telephone and cable services highly efficient, regular, and reliable.

The same superlatives apply to professional services of all kinds, and the fees for these services are kept very reasonable by vigorous competition.

English and Chinese are the official languages, and all official documentation is printed in both. Language presents no difficulty at all for a westerner.

The Hong Kong economy is very free enterprise oriented. There are no exchange controls, and the Hong Kong dollar (five to the U.S. dollar) circulates freely with all world currencies in a completely unregulated money market. The economically wide open nature of Hong Kong is a product of the political order. As a British crown colony, it has very limited independence. The governor, appointed by the Queen, nominates the two councils of government: The Executive Council (cabinet) and the Legislative Council. Unlike the crown colonies discussed earlier, there are no elections here. The cabinet members and the legislators are "opinion leaders" of the Chinese community. Almost to a man, they are economically conservative. No socialist scheme would find significant support in the government. Even if the government were inclined to socialism, there are solid practical reasons why it would not go far along the collectivist road. For example, the huge refugee population means that any form of government welfare would immediately destroy the colony, and thus such welfarism is inconceivable. The two councils, moreover, have very limited power vis á vis the governor. He nominates all their members, and so controls them indirectly. He also has the power to act against the majority opinions of the Executive Council, in which case his only responsibility is to the British secretary of state for foreign and commonwealth affairs. He even has direct legislative powers, and there is a long tradition of staunchly conservative governors in Hong Kong.

The legal system is based on British common law, modified by local law. The court system is British in structure.

Hong Kong has preserved the nineteenth century spirit of free enterprise to an extent that is surprising in this day and age. Taxes are progressive, but the top bracket is 17 percent of net income. There is a 15 percent annual tax on the rental value of land and buildings, with the exception of New Territories lands and buildings and owner-occupied land. There is a salary tax that tops out at 15 percent on net income, a similar profits tax with a 17 percent maximum, and a tax on bank-deposit interest (17 percent maximum), provided the rate of interest is more than 4 percent a year. All these taxes apply only to locally generated income. There are no taxes on capital, gifts, or capital gains, and death duties, which apply to assets physically located in Hong

Kong, are imposed in progressive brackets up to a maximum of 15 percent. There is no tax on dividends of local corporations. The official reason for this is that if the source of profit is local business, then the company has already been taxed on its profits and there is no justification for taxing the stockholders. As for foreign-source income, the idea of taxing this is unthinkable. A corollary of the happy lack of dividend taxes is no withholding tax on dividends. One can receive the profits of a Hong Kong corporation, dealing outside Hong Kong, in, say, Costa Rica without any Hong Kong tax liability of any kind. A final tax advantage is that the United States recognizes any taxes paid to Hong Kong as credit against U.S. tax liabilities.

Apart from the above taxes, government revenue in Hong Kong derives from duties on "luxury" commodities such as tobacco and alcohol, minor fees on imports and exports, and stamp duties. The latter apply to transfers of shares (HK $.80 for each HK $100), promissory notes and bills of exchange (HK $.25 for each HK $1,000), and mortgages and debentures (HK $2.00 for each HK $1,000).

Now, what about incorporation and trust formation in Hong Kong? As usual, articles of incorporation and association are required, and they must include the standard information. All these requirements are pure formalities, because nominees can be used for everything. In view of the labor situation in Hong Kong, $100 (U.S.) a year will cover a nominee director who is at the same time a registered shareholder as well as a company officer. There is no scarcity of law and trust firms to handle all the details.

Annual maintenance of a corporation involves annual auditing, signed by a chartered accountant, submitted to all shareholders, with a copy to the government. This is required because of the taxation of local income; all corporations must be audited to make certain that no such profits are concealed. A local representative can take care of the audit, keep the company seal, display the company name on a sign in his office, and do whatever else is necessary.

What are the costs? The government charges are very low, $80 (U.S.) for registration and incorporation and $5 annual stamp duty. The initial expenses of incorporation, articles of association, and stock certificates, and the various uses of nominees can total as little as $230 (U.S.). Annual maintenance can be as low as $130. Bargains, to say the least.

Incorporation takes up to four weeks to accomplish. It can be done with complete privacy through nominee shareholders, for there is no legal requirement that ultimate beneficiary owners be disclosed.

The Hong Kong common law tradition also allows for trusts. The costs run about $200 for trust formation and $50 a year to keep things running. A Hong Kong trust pays no taxes on overseas investments and can enjoy the advantages of the free currency market.

A popular Hong Kong combination is coupling a trust with holding companies. This may allow that the benefits to beneficiaries be deferred much beyond the legal period of allowed perpetuity for the trust, thus permitting a much greater growth of the initial investment. The way this works is to have the trust own the stock of holding companies. When the trust fully matures, the beneficiaries will receive the stock of the holding companies rather than money. The holding companies themselves may be so set up as to pay dividends only after many more additional years, using all the extra time to enhance growth by completely tax-free reinvestment of profits. Another beneficial aspect of Hong Kong trusts is that there are no stamp duties on the transfer of investments if they are outside Hong Kong, which makes a trust-holding company arrangement free of stamp duty to the trust beneficiaries. Finally, as in the Bahamas, the local trust law allows for a "Cuba clause," which means that a Hong Kong trust can be used with no worries about the political future of the colony.

Just as Panama came out with flying colors as compared with even the Caymans, so Hong Kong, in certain ways, comes out with respect to Panama. There is business justification unlimited, at lower local tax and corporation costs and with similar privacy. On the other hand, the exclusion of bearer shares, the need for annual auditing, and the distance from the United States may be considered negative factors by some.

Liberia. The fact that Liberia is in Africa may put some readers off. Exposure to African news over the last twenty-five years causes many people to automatically associate the "Dark Continent" with immense political and social instability. Revolutions, tribal wars, pogroms against nonblacks, crazy dictators, coups—all these make Africa seem an unlikely haven for anything.

Liberia is a definite exception. It is not a recently

founded decolonialized "republic," subject to the whims of its new rulers and to Communist infiltration. It is the oldest black republic on the continent, founded in 1847 (twenty-five years after the country was first established in 1822) and stable for 132 years. Its founders were repatriated American blacks, who settled the country with the aid of American colonization societies. Not surprisingly, the model followed by the founders of the Liberian Republic was the nineteenth century United States, and the government is based on an adaptation of the United States Constitution. Unfortunately, as the U.S. Congress and Supreme Court have done their best to transform a constitution of freedom into a justification for welfare socialism, so the Liberian Congress and Supreme Court have not left the original constitution intact. Liberia is not a total tax haven; rather, it is a tax haven only for persons or corporations intending to derive income purely from external sources.

Liberia lies on the African west coast. Its total area of 43,000 square miles contains about 2 million persons. Its major exports are primary resources and agricultural products: rubber, high quality iron ore, diamonds, palm kernels, and coffee. There is some industrialization in the initial processing of both iron and rubber, making Liberia more advanced industrially than other black African states. The country has a very favorable trade balance because imports are much less extensive than exports.

Investors enjoy a truly unregulated free enterprise economy. Liberia has a large network of consular and diplomatic connections around the world. Transportation is tolerable. There is a modern freeport at Monrovia, the capital, served by major shipping lines from the U.S., Europe, and the Far East. There is good internal water transportation through a system of ports used for coastal and internal trade. The international airport at Robertsfield, near Monrovia, is served by regular, though infrequent, flights from the United States. Telecommunication and airmail are reliable, and English is the official language.

As we have noted, the Liberian government is modeled on that of the United States. There is a directly elected president, and the national legislature is bicameral, with a senate and a house of representatives.

Professional services are quite good, and many important international firms are competently represented. An important economic advantage of Liberia is that it uses the U.S. dollar as its official currency, and it circulates freely with locally coined metal currency denominated at less than one dollar. As in Hong Kong and Panama, there are no exchange controls.

Liberia taxes local residents on their worldwide incomes and corporations that are more than 50 percent locally owned or that earn their incomes from local sources. A Liberian corporation cannot help a Liberian citizen escape Liberian taxes on his foreign income. However, it can help non-Liberians. Foreigners who incorporate in Liberia and trade outside Liberia, even if the line of business is shipping and the ships fly the Liberian flag and use the facilities of Liberian ports, have no taxes to worry about.

The last comment is imprecise if "worry" is taken in the broad sense. There is an ambiguity in the local tax rules that permits, in principle, a withholding tax on dividends paid by Liberian domiciled companies to their overseas stockholders. This depends on an interpretation of a clause that is never used under the current official policy of cultivating the tax haven industry. Of course, the policy could be reversed, but this is most unlikely. As against this theoretical worry, there is a practical advantage. If one incorporates in Liberia but derives all his income from outside it, no annual returns to the government concerning corporate finances are required.

Incorporation in Liberia is not very different from incorporation in any other tax haven. There is a Liberian trust company with international representation. Its New York office can be used to arrange all local formalities without any major expense. Corporate law is modeled on Delaware corporate law. There are no domicile requirements for anybody associated with the company, so there is no need for nominee directors, officers, or shareholders. There is no requirement for locally held stockholders' or directors' meetings, etc. There is even no necessity for a locally registered office. No documents need to be kept anywhere in Liberia, and no local office has to be decorated with a sign emblazoned with the name of the company. The only necessary kind of local representation is that needed for initial incorporation. Bearer shares are legally recognized, and it is possible to buy, "off the shelf," an already extant company from a trust organization. Since such a "shelf corporation" is controlled through bearer shares, no registration of ultimate ownership need be made anywhere. These "ready-made" corporations can even be bought from a trust company through an agent, further enhancing the privacy of the arrangement.

All this may sound good, but what is even better is the speed and the cost. To incorporate a new company based on a "model charter" takes only forty-eight hours from the time the process is begun in New York. If a special charter is required, the forty-eight hours begins the moment the papers reach Liberia. When incorporation has been effected, a cable is sent to the incorporator informing him that he is in business.

Despite all these advantages, Liberian incorporation is quite inexpensive. The government takes $100 on capital plus a $15 stamp duty, for a total of $115. The trust company representative in New York takes $500 in fees the first year, including $150 as an advance payment to the local agent. Annual maintenance runs $150 for representation, plus a government registration fee of $100. All told, incorporation costs $615 plus annual maintenance of $250. Few places can offer better prices. There is a requirement for $500 in paid-up capital at the time of incorporation, but this can be bypassed through the purchase of an off-the-shelf company. Part of the trust company costs are justified by the need for three original incorporators (proxies) to sign the certificate of incorporation.

The required articles of incorporation are fairly standard. They must include: (1) The name of the company, including a designation indicating its corporate, limited-liability character. (2) Capitalization: a statement of the maximum number of shares of capital stock the company is authorized to issue. This can be amended later. Shares may or may not have par value; they may be stated in any currency;

they can be marketed at any rate the company's board of directors decides as long as it is not less than par value, if any; they can be registered or bearer shares (the latter must be paid up in full); they can be voting or nonvoting; etc. (3) A specification of whether or not the company is to terminate its existence and be liquidated after a pre-specified number of years. (4) Domicile. This is standard: Monrovia, Liberia. The address of the business agent resident in Monrovia must be stated, together with his name. There is no implication in this, however, that his office is thereby the "locally registered office" of the corporation, and no unneeded formality such as the corporate name hanging in his office is required. (5) The names and addresses of at least three directors. These are supplied by the trust company at no charge, and they resign automatically once the incorporation goes through. No further official notification of who are the new directors is required. The law also allows stating that the number of directors is variable between a minimum of three and whatever maximum is desired. (6) The names of three original incorporators. The trust company will supply these three, who will revert their share certificates once incorporation is complete. (7) Indemnity clauses specifying whether or not persons authorized to represent the corporation to third parties are or are not indemnified by the company for legal costs arising from suits they might face as a result of their acting on behalf of the corporation. If so, the extent of indemnification must be specified. (8) Officers. A corporation must have a president, a secretary, and a treasurer authorized to represent it to third parties, and all three offices can be held by one person. If proxies are used for incorporation, there is no legal requirement to inform the government who their replacements are. (9) Other clauses specifying the scope and nature of corporate activities. This is strictly up to the incorporator, the only restriction being that no illegal activities be included.

If one wants to register a ship in Liberia, this should be done through this Liberian corporation. The extra costs on the ship, apart from incorporation, are $725 plus one cent per ton. The fixed charge is higher than in Panama, but on the other hand, the cost per ton is lower.

The situation for trusts is not nearly as favorable as that for incorporation. Liberia's legal system is fundamentally American in its principles. However, the application of these principles by the courts is quite different. Instead of the common law tradition of legal interpretation, Liberian interpretation is similar to the European civil law approach: constitutional principles are applicable directly, on the basis of the understanding of the judge applying them, with no special regard for precedent. Thus, the precedent-based legal framework offered by the common law is missing, and, with it, the advisability of Liberian trusts.

Costa Rica. In the first part of this book, we discussed certain approaches and possibilities offered by tax havens to enhance the growth of saved investments by eliminating or reducing the annual tax burden that inhibits their development. We have also discussed the need for making a decision concerning who is eventually to get the benefit of this and when. If one's heirs are the intended users, a trust is the proper instrument, possibly coupled with a holding company. If the investor is the intended user, then a corporation is what is needed.

But what happens when the time comes to establish direct legal entitlement to accumulated funds? Will this not require that one's corporation pay him a dividend that will be taxable as part of his income, albeit at what may be lower rates? Or, suppose the overseas corporation does not exhaust its accumulated income through dividend payments or liquidation. This means that all its accumulated assets will eventually become part of the owner's personal estate to the extent of his stock ownership. Thus his intended heirs will be hit by estate, probate, and death duties—unless the property is transferred through a trust. But this does not help the investor who wants to enjoy, eventually, the use of the accumulated wealth himself. What can he do?

The answer for some is immigration to a country that (1) gives U.S. citizens immediate immigration rights, (2) grants immigrants from the U.S. an immediate local passport, (3) exempts the foreign-generated income of a U.S. immigrant from any kind of taxes, and (4) is politically stable, economically comfortable, and culturally and socially pleasant to live in. Utopia? No, Costa Rica.

Costa Rican Law 4812 entitles any U.S. citizen to qualify for the status of *pensionado,* provided he has a guaranteed minimum monthly income of at least $500 plus $75 for each dependent over fifteen years old that he brings with him. This income must be verified by bank or other documentation. A pensionado has many advantages: no immigration tax, no tax on foreign-source income, no customs duties on his household goods to a value of $7,000 provided they are not sold or removed from the country within three years, no import duty on a family car provided it is not sold within five years, and the right to import a new car, duty-free, every five years. All this is immediately conjoined with all the rights of Costa Rican citizenship with the exception of voting rights. One of these rights is a Costa Rican passport.

Unlike most Latin American countries, Costa Rica is a genuine and stable democracy. Its president is directly elected for only one term of four years, after which he is ineligible for reelection. A professional, nonpolitical civil service manages many functions that in other countries are considered to require some sort of political control. Thus, to a large extent, what little government activity there is in the economy is independent of the politics of the day. And the economy is stable and prosperous.

One can easily go to Costa Rica and see it for himself before making any decision to immigrate. Situated in Central America between Nicaragua and Panama, it is just three hours from Miami by air, or it can be reached by car. It has Florida-like weather, abundant natural beauty, a friendly population, a low cost of living, and an American community of about 8,500 persons in the capital of San José alone. English is widely spoken, and the many schools for Spanish-language training are inexpensive. There are four color television channels, many radio stations, and a national theater featuring internationally renowned artists. The crime rate is low. The constitution expressly forbids a standing army, eliminating the danger of revolution and the expense of maintaining professional soldiers. Could one ask for more?

As for taxes, personal income tax does not apply to a pensionado living on foreign-source income. If one buys and sells shares of local companies, there are no capital gains taxes to bother with. If one owns a local company, however, a 15 percent withholding tax applies to dividends paid on bearer shares.

Although we are mainly interested in the use of Costa Rica as a tax haven, let us briefly discuss the investment possibilities. The stable political system, the security from war, the lack of a standing army, the sound legal system, the low crime rate, the abundance of skilled labor, and the open channels to the Central American Common Market mean that one can make good money by, say, investing in a partnership with a Costa Rican (under the law, he must have an interest of at least 50 percent). There are a number of special government-guaranteed advantages. Details are available from the Centro Para La Promocion de las Exportaciones y de las Inversionnes (Apartado 5418, San José, Costa Rica) and from The Information Center, Overseas Private Investment Corporation (Washington, DC 20257). The latter is a U.S. government agency that serves to encourage American investment in those countries where the U.S. is interested in enhancing prosperity.

Is it worth writing for information? Consider these general facts: (1) The Costa Rican Export Promotion Law eliminates import duty on imported goods that are used for the production of exportable goods. (2)

If one offers a significant investment and has both a successful track record and a project compatible with government development goals, he can get a loan or a guarantee for a U.S. loan through the Overseas Private Investment Corporation. (3) The OPIC provides insurance against loss due to expropriation, war damages, revolution, insurrection, and inconvertibility of funds. This insurance is available to U.S. individuals, U.S. corporations with at least 50 percent U.S. stock ownership, U.S. partnerships and associations with the same ownership requirement, and even foreign business entities with at least 95 percent ownership by an American entity.

One can invest in agriculture, industry, or tourism —that is, most anything. Of course, government readiness to grant privileges will depend on how much it considers an investment scheme to harmonize with its preferences. However, if one meets all requirements, he can look forward to Costa Rican tax exemptions (local and national) on domestically generated income.

Are there any investment limitations? In principle, one can invest in any industry apart from liquor production and insurance, both of which are nationalized in Costa Rica. But if he fails to have 90 percent local employees (apart from top executives and technical personnel, who may be foreigners), fails to channel at least 85 percent of his payroll to local employees, and fails to have a fully empowered local representative, he does not get any of the special privileges offered by the government. However, local labor is good, and unions are unheard of.

There are four distinct legal modes for organizing a Costa Rican company:

General Partnership. Both partners have full, unlimited liability for all company debts. If one intends to invest locally and trust his Costa Rican partner with running the business, he had best avoid a general partnership.

Limited Partnership. The foreign partner has limited liability, while the local partner, who runs the business, has full liability.

Corporation.

Limited Liability Company. These are partnerships with declared limited liabilities for each of the partners.

Incorporation in Costa Rica is not like that in Liberia or Hong Kong. There is no privacy, the company has to be recorded with the Commercial Registry, and a notification of its creation must be published in the official government gazette. The procedures are essentially the same as they are in other countries.

Investment and speculation in real estate is possible in Costa Rica. Although no special privileges are granted for this type of investment except in very special cases, there is no legal restriction on foreigners buying, owning, and selling real estate. There are some things that must be kept in mind, however:

(1) If a property borders on water, the first 50 meters from high tide cannot be titled and are automatically reserved for public use; the next 150 meters are controlled by the municipalities and the national government and cannot be privately owned (unless private title has already been established), though they can sometimes be leased.

(2) A condition for buying public land (as against land previously owned by individuals) is ten years of Costa Rican residence by the buyer.

(3) After ten years of Costa Rican residence, one can lease public land for agricultural purposes. The terms run from ten to twenty years, are not fixed in advance, and depend on crop yields. If the yield is very good, the chances are the lease will be short.

(4) Even on private land, mineral and subsoil rights remain with the government, though one can get a concession to use them. Similarly, forest reserves are regulated by the government even if privately owned.

(5) There may be legal problems if a purchaser does not make sure the seller has absolutely clear title. There is a local company that does title searches.

(6) The transfer of land requires public registration of a deed, and the sale is valid only if the preceding sale has been legally registered.

(7) Land bought by local small farmers from the Institute de Tierras y Colonizacion for agricultural use cannot be resold. One must verify with the institute that land offered for sale is not subject to this restriction.

(8) A legal sale is possible only after all real estate taxes due on the land have been fully paid. Thus, the seller must present an Internal Revenue Office receipt.

(9) Local law grants some partial ownership rights to "squatters" who have been using land for years without any official authorization.

But all this may be of little interest to the reader who is seeking a tax haven, not investment possibilities in the local economy. So here is how to go about removing to beautiful Costa Rica. First, write to the Retirees Club of Costa Rica, Apartado 8–3880, San José, Costa Rica. The club will provide much useful information. Then write to the immigration office in the Costa Rican embassy in Washington, specifying your name (including maternal surname), your profession or occupation, your present nationality, your purpose for desiring Costa Rican residence *(pensionado* status), the names and ages of those who will accompany you, your present address, and any other data you think pertinent. You will be answered in two or three weeks.

To get a visa, you will also need to present a valid U.S. passport, proof that you have the minimum required monthly income, your birth certificate, police certification of good conduct, three passport-size photos, and general health and smallpox vaccination certificates. When you are ready to go, you will also need a list of the household goods you are taking with you.

Bon voyage! I will probably meet you in San José when I retire.

NINE

Double-Taxation-Agreement Havens: Double Your Pleasure...

A U.S. taxpayer who pays tax on his investment returns as part of his personal income need not worry about the U.S. withholding tax. This applies only to U.S.-originated incomes—dividends, rent, interest on bonds (but not that on bank deposits), royalties—that are paid to a foreign legal entity. However, once one alienates his investment portfolio to such a foreign entity, either a corporation or a trust, he trades off the usual income tax for the 30 percent withholding tax, paid on the income at its U.S. source before it reaches the haven entity.

The withholding tax is not unqualified. A citizen of a foreign country would hardly be interested in investing in the United States if he had to pay such a tax on top of taxes imposed by his home country. Hence, the U.S. government, interested in encouraging foreigners to invest in America, has double-taxation agreements with many other nations. Such agreements usually include the following provisions: (1) Reduction of the U.S. withholding tax from 30 percent to 15 and sometimes 5 percent (if the foreign corporation involved owns 95 percent of the stock of the U.S. company from which it receives dividends). (2) Acceptance of the U.S. withholding tax as a credit against local tax liabilities. In other words, instead of taxing the 85 percent of the original dividend that remains after deducting U.S. withholding tax as if it were a gross income, the foreign investor's country treats the full amount of the original income as gross income, applies the local income tax, and reduces the tax due by the amount already paid to the United States. (3) A citizen of one of the countries party to the agreement who earns *all* his income in the other can pick which one he wants to pay his taxes to. (4) An agreement to exchange information to facilitate the capture of tax evaders.

Most double-taxation agreements are not of interest to someone seeking a tax haven. They are with highly industrialized, highly taxed countries. However, some double-taxation agreements between the United States and some West European countries apply to the overseas colonial territories of the European signatories, and these overseas territories have much lower tax rates than their mother countries. Investments in such havens bear a total tax burden equal to the sum of the reduced U.S. withholding tax (usually 5 percent) and the local tax on what remains from the U.S.-source income after deduction of the withholding tax or on the full original income with the U.S. tax accepted as a credit. If this sum is less than 30 percent, a corporation or trust in such a country is preferable to a "pure" haven entity.

The major hitch in setting up such a company or trust is avoiding Subpart F penalties. There are two ways to approach this problem. One can make everything pristinely legal, consulting a good tax lawyer who can advise him how to make his double-taxation-agreement outfit exempt from Subpart F. The other is to establish a corporation in a no-tax haven, which in turn establishes a corporation in the double-taxation-agreement haven. The legality of the latter approach is far from a certain thing. The corporation enjoying the benefits of the double-taxation agreement is not directly owned or controlled by a U.S.-resident citizen or company, but by a nonresident alien legal entity. And the creation of the second company is not something that must be reported to the IRS. Is this sort of arrangement illegal?

Such a double-tier setup might even be used to reduce the already low local tax burden of the company in the double-taxation haven. That company could pay, say, royalties to the no-tax corporation. These payments would reduce its *net* profit on the books and, thus, the local taxes it must pay. And, of course, the no-tax corporation will have nothing to pay on its royalty income. If the royalties eat up all the income of the double-taxation corporation, no net taxable income is left.

Of course, one must weigh the advantages of this kind of arrangement against the costs of an extra corporation. Is 10–12.5 percent of one's annual investment return more or less than the costs of incorporating and maintaining a company? Clearly, a portfolio has to be rather large to justify the extra

171

expense. With these thoughts firmly in mind, let us now consider the double-taxation havens.

The Netherlands Antilles. The Netherlands Antilles is a confederation of six islands, consisting of two groups of three islands each. The Windward Islands (St. Maarten, St. Eustatius, Saba) are situated about 40 miles east of Puerto Rico. The Leeward Islands (Aruba, Curacao, and Bonaire) are 600 miles to the southwest of the Windwards; Curacao is 40 miles north of the Venezuelan coast. The islands are tropical, but their climate is made pleasant by the northeast tradewinds. The average temperature is a bit over eighty-one degrees Fahrenheit with only very slight deviations, and the average humidity is about 75 percent.

The total land area is about 400 square miles. Most of the population of 240,000 is concentrated on Curacao, the major island. Curacao is a very popular tourist resort, a freeport, and a financial center in which major international banking firms and large oil refining companies are represented. The principal languages of the islands are Dutch, Spanish, English, and Papiamento (a native language).

Sea and air transport to the islands are acceptable, and so is interisland marine transport. Communication by phone, cable, telex, and airmail is good, both to the islands and among them.

The Netherlands Antilles are one of the two partners of the Kingdom of the Netherlands, together with continental Holland. Internally, the Antilles have complete political autonomy. Defense and foreign policy are established and supported by the

Dutch parliament, and executed by the Dutch cabinet, supplemented by ministerial representatives from the Antilles. The U.S.–Holland double-taxation agreement extends to the Netherlands Antilles, and internal taxation is determined by the local legislature.

There are two levels of local government, "municipal" and "federal." At the municipal level, there are four separate island territories: Aruba, Curacao, Bonaire, and the Windward Islands, each of which has its own council presided over by a lieutenant governor appointed directly by the Queen of Holland. In each case, the lieutenant governor presides over an administrative board, which consists of members of the local council. The federal level comprises a queen-appointed governor and a council of ministers, responsible to an elected legislature. The relationship between the two levels of government is similar to that between the states and federal government of the United States. However, the physical separation of the four areas making up the confederation gives the relative independence of each area enhanced significance. The legal tradition of the Antilles is derived from the continental Dutch system, and is, consequently, that of the civil law, which makes establishment of a trust impossible.

Professional services are limited. There are a few notaries and public auditors. There are some banks in Curacao.

Unfortunately, exchange controls are strict. One is supposed to use the local currency, the Netherlands Antilles guilder. Investment companies, patent-holding companies, and companies with no local dealings, local ownership, or local business partners can obtain an exemption from this rule.

Before we discuss local tax law and the double-taxation agreement with the United States, let us survey the relevant features of local incorporation. The incorporation documents must be executed before a notary. There are but seven notaries in the whole of the Netherlands Antilles, four of whom are in Curacao. The local law gives a notary the exclusive right to handle such matters, and he can prepare the documentation as well.

There is only one basic document, the articles of incorporation, which covers the matters ordinarily dealt with in articles of association. The documentation for incorporation must be approved, in draft or final form, by the local minister of justice. This takes from ten days to a few weeks. The documentation must be in Dutch, though a sworn English translation can be made.

Both the articles of incorporation and minister's "decrees of no objection" are published in an official gazette, and companies are registered in the public commercial register.

At least one company director must be a local resident, and by law, each director is entitled to bind the corporation contractually to third parties unless otherwise specified in the articles of incorporation. A company may have, but is not obliged to have, a body of "overseers."

The name of the corporation must include "NV," the Dutch equivalent of "Inc." or "Ltd." Shares must have par value and voting rights. Bearer shares are allowed, but some shares must be registered. The authorized capital need not be fixed, and a corporation is allowed to buy back shares, cancel them, and thus reduce its capital. At least twenty percent of the authorized capital must be paid in *at all times,* not just at the time of incorporation. Even if shares have been redeemed and canceled, 20 percent of the new, reduced authorized capital must still be paid in.

Finally, local meetings of shareholders are required. Apart from this, if all shareholders are registered, a unanimously supported written circular signed by all shareholders is a legally approved form for reaching company decisions.

All these unpleasant requirements have their cost. A "shelf company," already incorporated and approved, can be purchased for $1,200–$1,500 and maintained for $600–$1,000 a year. The maintenance costs cover furnishing a local office with an appropriate nameplate, paying a local managing director (proxy), holding annual shareholders' meetings, and filing tax returns. There is a Cuba clause for corporations. Corporate assets can be transferred to those countries that have a similar law and allow such transfers: Holland, Switzerland, Surinam, and some Canadian provinces.

Now, here is the local tax situation. The Netherlands Antilles, like the United States, taxes the worldwide income of a corporation, not just locally generated income. The corporate income tax ranges from 2.7 to 40 percent on the federal level, averaging about 27–34 percent for most companies. In addition, there is a 15 percent municipal surtax.

The above rates apply only to "general" corporations. There are certain activities that put a company in one of several different categories. Investment companies pay a 2.4 percent tax on the first $50,000 in profits and 3 percent thereafter. Holding companies that hold stocks, patents, trademarks, copyrights, rights to motion pictures, and real estate are subject to a flat 3 percent tax. Shipping companies pay taxes of up to 10 percent.

There is neither a dividends tax nor a withholding tax. Dividends transferred out of the Antilles are not taxed. Also, there are no tax liabilities on capital gains, on dividends and interest from investment and holding companies, and no inheritance or estate taxes.

Now we come to what makes the Netherlands Antilles important: the double-taxation agreement with the United States. The basic treaty was concluded by the U.S. and the Netherlands in 1948 and extended to the Antilles in 1955. This original treaty reduced the U.S. withholding tax for Antilles corporations to 15 percent on dividends and to zero on most interest and royalties. This, combined with a 3 percent local tax meant a maximum 18 percent tax on dividends and 3 percent on interest and royalties.

In 1963, when the U.S. Congress added Subpart F to the tax code, the treaty was amended. Its relevant provisions for our purposes are: (1) Income derived from U.S. real estate (rent) or as interest from mortgages secured by U.S. real estate is taxed according to U.S. rates in the U.S. and exempted from Antilles taxation. (2) Dividends paid by a U.S. corporation to Antilles shareholders are taxed by the U.S. at 15 percent unless the Antilles shareholders own at least 95 percent of the U.S. corporation making the payment, in which case the rate is 5 percent. (3) Interest paid by a U.S. corporation to an Antilles company is fully exempt from U.S. tax if the deal is made at more than "arm's length" and the Antilles corporation holds less than 50 percent of the American company; if Antilles ownership is 50 percent or more, interest is fully taxed. (4) Royalties of all kinds derived by an Antilles corporation from a U.S. corporation are fully exempted from the U.S. withholding tax. (5) If an Antilles corporation derives rental income from U.S. sources it has the option of being taxed in the U.S. or locally in any given year. (6) An Antilles company electing to enjoy all the above benefits must agree to pay the Antilles authorities the normal tax on its net annual profit. One cannot combine the advantages of a 3 percent local tax with a withholding tax reduction. This is an unfortunate hitch, but it still gives one the benefit of paying 15 percent of full profits and the Antilles tax on 85 percent of full profits. This saving on withholding tax can be increased by reducing the net income of the Antilles corporation through payments (rent, dividends, interest, etc.) to some other tax haven corporation. (7) Similarly, if a corporation elects to enjoy the total reduction of withholding tax on interest and royalties, it must be ready to pay a local tax of 24 percent on its net income up to $56,000 and 30 percent beyond that.

Thus, any tax savings in the Netherlands Antilles depend on the nature of the investments included in the portfolio transferred to the Antilles company. Bonds and debentures, copyrights, interest, etc., will carry no withholding tax, but will be hit by a 24 percent local tax on the net, which means a maximum total of 24 percent. Interest on mortgages is taxed 30 percent U.S. withholding *plus* a local 24 percent tax on the net. Interest on bank deposits is generally immune from the U.S. withholding tax, so, if deposits are owned by an Antilles company, the only tax levied is the local one.

There is one further aspect of the Netherlands Antilles that is of some slight interest. It has a freeport similar to the Colon Free Zone. It allows companies to import goods, pack and process them locally, and reexport them exempt from duty and one-third of the profits tax, provided nothing is sold locally.

The British Virgin Islands. The British Virgin Islands, like the Netherlands Antilles, inherited their double-taxation agreement with the United States from a similar agreement between a colonial mother country (in this case, Great Britain) and the U.S.

But, first, let us look at the islands themselves. There are sixty of them, located some sixty miles east of Puerto Rico. Their total land area is 69 square miles. Only a few of the islands are inhabited, among them Tortola (21 square miles), Virgin Gorda (8.3), Jost Van Dyke (3.5), and Anegada (15). The BVI form one economic-social unit with the U.S. Virgin Islands (St. Thomas, St. John, and St. Croix).

The local climate is subtropical, moderated by the tradewinds. Temperatures range from the low seventies to the low eighties on the average, and there are substantial rains and an occasional hurricane. The hilly, picturesque terrain offers many attractions to tourists.

The BVI can be reached by air through Puerto Rico, and there is good steamship service. The islands are well-connected to each other and the U.S. Virgins by commercial boat. Airmail, cable, telephone, and telex operate between the BVI and the U.S. Direct-dial telephone from the U.S. began in 1978.

The islands are a British colony. A governor appointed by the Queen of England handles foreign affairs, defense, justice and legal matters, internal security, civil service, and finance. On all other matters he is bound constitutionally by the advice of his executive council. The latter is comprises himself as chairman, the chief minister, the attorney general, the financial secretary, and two other ministers. The latter two are appointed by the governor on the advice of the chief minister and are confirmed by majority vote of the Legislative Council. The latter consists of a speaker, the attorney general, the financial secretary, one member appointed by the governor, and seven popularly elected members. Thus, while the BVI is a democracy, the vote of the general population has a very limited effect on government affairs. The governor has both very large direct responsibilities and indirect powers derived from his control over the two councils. The legal system is British common law. There are some local laws restricting land purchases by aliens. The language is English.

The common law tradition, the language, the fact that the local currency is the U.S. dollar, and the lack of any exchange controls favor the BVI over the Netherlands Antilles. Another advantage of the BVI is the relatively extensive professional services available: four commercial banks and numerous accountants and lawyers. There is an independent trust company, the British-American Trust Company Limited.

More important, local rates are better than those of the Antilles. The corporate income tax is 15 percent on net income. The individual income tax is progressive, 4–12 percent of income after an exemption of 5 percent. This tax is imposed on worldwide income. There are no capital, capital gains, sales, or death taxes. Import duties range from 5 to 20 percent. A thirty-five cent stamp duty applies to all bills of exchange, but not to checks. There is a 2.5 percent estate-transfer duty applicable to stock as well as to real estate. Some "approved" industries are totally tax exempt. For example, hotels and pioneer industries are granted ten-year exemptions.

Local incorporation is cheap and easy, and so is maintenance of a company by a local agent. We will skip the details this time, but as against the Netherlands Antilles, there are no special costs or requirements.

We now come to the double-taxation agreement. Withholding tax on dividends from the U.S. is 15 percent to any BVI corporation if it is both taxed in the BVI and is not involved in any regular trade or business in the U.S. through a permanent establishment in the U.S. (such as a management office). The corporation must be "managed and controlled" through a BVI office. If the BVI corporation effectively owns the U.S. company (95 percent ownership or more), the withholding tax is reduced to 5 percent. A BVI corporation that is fully taxed in the BVI is fully exempt from U.S. withholding tax on royalties, whatever their source. A BVI corporation is fully exempt from U.S. tax on capital gains. It is also exempt locally since there is no BVI capital gains tax. There is no U.S. tax on profits earned by ships registered in the BVI. A BVI company that owns real estate in the U.S. can elect to be taxed by the United States as a nonresident alien, paying 15 percent withholding tax on rent but paying no capital gains tax. The 15 percent U.S. withholding tax is allowed as a tax credit against the 15 percent BVI tax, thus eliminating BVI tax if all income has been taxed by the U.S.

Clearly, the BVI is preferable to the Netherlands Antilles on all counts. Incorporation is easier and cheaper, local taxes are lower, and withholding tax concessions are better.

Barbados. Is there any tax haven that offers the advantages of a double-taxation agreement plus virtually no local taxes? Incredibly, there is: Barbados. How long this will last is hard to say. Things may change as soon as the IRS sees this book.

Barbados, which lies just east of the Windwards, is a former English colony; thus it enjoys all the advantages of the double-taxation agreement detailed above for the BVI. It has a 40 percent corporate tax, but wait a minute . . . An "international business company," a corporation owned and controlled by nonresidents and doing business exclusively outside Barbados is taxed differently. It pays no tax on profits of trade and manufacture and only 2.5 percent on investment returns. The fact that such a company is subject to a local tax, however small, means that the double-taxation agreement applies to it. The U.S. dividend withholding tax goes from 30 percent to 15 percent (or 5 percent, as above). Royalty taxes go to zero, and so on. If part of the profit is transferred abroad as dividends to nonresident stockholders, a 2.5 percent Barbados withholding tax applies.

TEN

Liechtenstein: A Bit of Utopia in Old Europe

The reader may wonder what else there is to discuss, what other categories of tax havens can exist apart from those already covered. Liechtenstein logically falls in the category of foreign-source-income havens, but it has certain features that merit special attention. In addition to "standard" corporate entities, it offers certain other possibilities. These can provide many of the benefits of corporations and trusts in flexible combination, almost "to order," without many of the disadvantages of both usual forms.

There is one important caveat to keep in mind, however: IRS officials have a very deeply entrenched conditioned reflex of vast suspicion toward any business related to Liechtenstein. They "know" tax evasion is involved. Thus, it is better to use a Liechtensteinian entity indirectly, through at least one intermediary entity.

Another preliminary point about Liechtenstein that must be mentioned is that it is a civil law country, not a common law one. Its legal tradition has considerable Swiss-German ancestry. Thus, one would not expect trust-like entities to be possible. But, surprisingly, they are.

Unlike most other tax havens, Liechtenstein is not geographically isolated. It is a tiny principality on the banks of the Rhine, sandwiched between Austria and Switzerland. It is 16 miles long and, on the average, 3.7 miles wide. It is indirectly accessible by air. One can fly to Zürich and drive from there, or fly to any other European capital and go from there by train. The telecommunication and airmail services are excellent. Satellite direct-dialing makes telephone communication extremely easy.

Politically, Liechtenstein is a constitutional monarchy. Legal sovereignty is exercised cooperatively and wisely by a hereditary prince and a democratically elected parliament. The tiny nation is very stable and prosperous, economically and socially.

Liechtenstein is now heavily industrialized, though not long ago it was mainly agricultural. It is economically united with Switzerland. There are no customs barriers separating the two countries, and their joint currency is the rock-solid Swiss franc.

The legal code has an interesting history. It originated in Austro-Hungarian law. In 1914, local legislation amending this basic law began to be enacted, influenced by both the German legal tradition and Swiss property law. In 1926 a unique, locally originated code dealing with property of both "physical" and "juridical" persons was drawn up. This code is the third chapter of a more general locally developed code of civil law. It defines various forms of available legal personalities—the "establishment," the "foundation," the company limited by shares, and the trust—and relates the defined entities to tax law.

The most important feature of this law from a tax haven point of view is that a holding company, a company whose main purpose is the management of property and participation in other business organizations or the permanent management of holdings in other business organizations, is exempt from capital and earnings (income) taxes. Such a company pays an annual tax of 0.1 percent of its total paid-up capital and reserve.

A similar tax immunity is granted to "domiciled" companies, companies defined not by reference to the specific nature of their business activities but by reference to their noninvolvement in local business. Again, a tax of 0.1 percent of total paid-up capital plus reserves is payable by such companies.

Even better tax treatment is granted to "foundations," which, as against companies limited by shares (essentially standard corporations), are unique local creations. Foundations enjoy special sliding tax rates on capital. They are also exempt from the requirement of registration in the commercial register, thereby combining the advantages of privacy with that of virtually no taxes. There are two basic kinds of foundations. Family foundations are granted the tax benefits of the sliding rate scale on all capital over 10 million Swiss francs. Ordinary foundations enjoy these benefits on everything above 2 million francs.

Another advantage of Liechtenstein is its bank secrecy. In fact, Liechtenstein preserves the Swiss tradition better than Switzerland. It enforces bank secrecy laws with great severity and is in no way committed internationally to relax these laws. This, combined with its lack of exchange controls, the world's strongest currency, unique corporate and tax laws, and excellent professional services, make Liechtenstein very attractive indeed.

All these advantages, however, do not favor Liechtenstein over, say, Hong Kong. What merits it a special place in our considerations are the unique legal entities, the foundation and the establishment.

The best way to understand the former is as a variation of the trust. It can be set up to allocate future property, generated by the investment of an original endowment, to family members or other beneficiaries. Instead of a trustee, there is a board (usually provided by a local trust company) that manages the principal fund (the endowment) and makes grants to the intended beneficiaries out of the returns on the investment, out of the principal invested, or both.

A foundation need not be limited to such trustlike functions. It can, in principle, simply manage one's estate with the distinct advantage of untaxable returns derived by a separate legal person. A foundation is not locally taxable if it is mainly involved in investment in other companies or if it has no local business involvements apart from its own management.

The question of Subpart F liability is interesting. If a taxpayer reports a Liechtensteinian foundation, the IRS might refuse to recognize it as a proper corporate entity and tax all its income as though it were his. But since the foundation is a legal form not reducible to either the corporation or the trust, despite its partial similarity to both, a taxpayer would legally, at least by the letter of the law, never have to report any involvement with one. If by some chance such involvement came to light, he should be fully covered against criminal charges. No personal income would have been concealed, because the foundation, a legal entity in its own right, is distinct from its settler and earns its own income. There would be no question of a failure to report involvement in the formation of a foreign corporation or trust because neither of these legal entities would have been involved.

To return to the nature of foundations, the most prominent type is the straight family foundation, designed to support family members, provide for their education, etc. A mixed family foundation is similar, only it serves to provide for members of other families as well. The establishment of a foundation requires the separation of the endowment, constituting the foundation's property, from the estate of the settler and giving it a special name, purpose, and internal organization. It is these legal acts that give the foundation its "legal personality." Because this legal personality is not constituted by state registration, a foundation can be validly constituted in a private manner.

Apart from the foundation's property (its endowment), a basic document signed by the settler, called the memorandum of settlement, is required. It is here that privacy may be compromised because the settler must sign and the signature must be officially certified. This can be taken care of by establishing a foundation through another legal person (such as a tax haven corporation) or through a lawyer with power of attorney, thus maintaining privacy.

The memorandum of foundation must specify: (1) name of the foundation, (2) domicile of the foundation, (3) objects and purposes of the foundation, which can be quite vague and general, (4) specification of the nature and amount of the endowment, (5) organization of the foundation, and (6) how the property of the foundation is to be finally distributed, to what beneficiaries, in what manner, under what conditions, and when the foundation is to be dissolved.

Clearly, this is quite similar to a trust deed. But there is a special local flexibility: the document, apart from meeting these requirements, can contain anything one wishes. Moreover, the discussion of the constitution of the foundation can be set forth in a separate document that also specifies the articles of settlement. Such a separate document would require another certified signature of the settler.

Still another legal possibility is to have a letter of settlement, specifying the terms of the settlement and empowering the foundation board or any third party to specify details about benefits, modes of distribution, and so on. This approach is advisable only for a testamentary foundation, applying after the settler's death, for it means foregoing the power to make decisions and changes on such issues.

One can specify the beneficiaries in extreme detail, or be quite general. It is also possible to have separate by-laws supplementary to the memorandum and the articles of settlement added at any time after the foundation is set up, specifying beneficiaries and benefits. Moreover—and this is the major advantage of a foundation—the founder can at any later time change his mind about any specific provision. Unlike a trust, under which one can only send a "memorandum of wishes" to the trustees which they can follow or ignore as they choose, a foundation allows one continued control without liability for foundation debts or taxes.

The various items that must be included in the basic document defining a foundation are as follows:

Name. The name of the foundation can be virtually whatever one chooses, provided it includes no national designations and does include either *Stiftung* ("foundation") or *Familienstiftung* ("family foundation") as its last word. Moreover, the name must involve nothing illegal or immoral and should not conflict with the name of any other existing foundation. Similarly, if one wants to set up a business foundation, it is impermissible to call it a family foundation, and vice versa. It is possible to establish a family foundation with business involvements as a subsidiary function if one so chooses, but the original and principal purpose of a foundation whose name includes "family foundation" must be the support of one's family. Still, if unforeseen circumstances make the primary purpose obsolete, no change of name is required.

The Purpose of the Foundation. This is generally similar for all: the administration of property and the distribution of income derived from that property. It can involve accumulation of property by self-insurance. The statement of purpose cannot include profit making as an independent objective. This does not mean that a foundation is barred from making, accumulating, and reinvesting profits for a given time—but this is the means, not the end. The end of a foundation, its proper and legitimate purpose, is to support beneficiaries. The point is that the foundation is trustlike in having a limited perpetuity period, at the end of which money must be distributed. It cannot go on making money indefinitely.

Apart from this general consideration, the statement of purpose can be as vague and general or as specific as desired. The details can be left to the foundation board, and when it comes to investment policies, the wisest course is to leave this to the managers. To formulate a business policy for decisions that may take place twenty-five years after the settler's death would be extremely unwise. What is important is to have some basic guidelines and competent managers.

The distribution of the foundation proceeds should be as specific as possible. If one wants to take care of his great-grandchildren yet unborn, a general description of this category of individuals is needed. One simple possibility is having a maintenance foundation paying a specified portion of its income to specified individuals without any extra set conditions or purposes. If, however, conditions or purposes are spelled out, they must be both legal and moral.

The Capital Requirement. This is the strictest requirement of all. Capital of the value of at least 20,000 Swiss francs must be irreversibly transferred to the foundation. If the assets do not consist of cash, one must provide proof by competent and independent assessment that their total value does not fall below the minimum paid-in capital limit.

Moreover, if the assets include IOUs, these IOUs can later be legally enforced on the settler by the beneficiaries.

There is a bright side to the irrevocable alienation. The foundation's capital is not any longer the settler's, and his creditors cannot make claims against it. Nor can the creditors of the foundation make claims against the settler. This may be important if one is the sole beneficiary of his foundation and he goes bankrupt. He can still enjoy the fruits of the foundation without any creditor access to the property; at most, they could make claims against benefits from the foundation, but not the foundation's assets.

The Organization of the Foundation. This constitutes the specification of foundation governing bodies. The settler can appoint them directly or appoint someone, such as the executor of his will, to appoint them. The first element is the "supreme authority." This is the settler. He determines the use and ultimate allocation of the foundation property. He appoints the original board members and can retain the right of dismissing them at will and appointing replacements. He establishes the beneficiaries, decides the distribution of benefits, etc. He can even maintain the right to revoke the foundation, amend its memorandum, add or delete new by-laws, or finally liquidate, dissolve, or merge the foundation with remaining property reverting to himself, to the beneficiaries, or to whomever he chooses. These extreme powers of "legislation" allow him to maintain day-to-day control over both the use of the money and its ultimate enjoyment, spared from the liabilities inherent in the normal management of personal property. He can make all investment decisions himself, make himself sole beneficiary, and still not be personally liable for taxes on the income the foundation earns or for whatever debts it may incur. Thus, one can have the advantages of a corporation coupled with those of a trust, and with complete privacy.

One caution: As has been noted, the Subpart F situation of foundations is uncertain. Existing IRS rulings do not explicitly refer to Liechtensteinian foundations, nor is it easy to classify a foundation as a specific subtype of the types of foreign business entities to which they do refer. So one can *probably* use this as a legal justification for keeping the existence and operation of a foundation strictly private, but this is something to be taken up with a very good tax lawyer.

The second element of foundation organization is the board. The terms of settlement of the foundation must specify how the board is appointed, how its members are dismissed, how a vacated position of a resigned board member is refilled. These decisions can be transferred to the board itself, reserved to the settler, or vested in whatever third party the settler chooses, including the beneficiaries. In the latter case, one must be specific about whether or not one of the beneficiaries can be appointed or elected a member of the board by other beneficiaries; if this is permitted, the method of doing so must be spelled out.

There is a legal presumption in foundation law that if authority to nominate board members and the authority to dismiss them are not explicitly separated, these two powers are united in one person or body, but the settler can leave to himself the right of dismissal and allow the board (including the dismissed member in his last act of involvement with the foundation) to elect the replacement member.

Obviously, board members cannot be nominated without their consent, and they can resign at any time. However, their initial consent to serve implies that they have to continue on the board until replaced. Alternatively, one can allow the board to act in the absence of a resigned member.

The functions of the board are similar to those of a trustee of a trust or, more accurately, to that of a corporate board of directors. They decide on the administration of investments and the distribution of benefits. The settler can, however, restrict the board's range of powers as he thinks best.

Board decisions are put into effect by majority vote, binding the minority, but even this "normal" feature can be altered in the terms of settlement. Any way one does it, though, the board's functions are administration and management. Any employee empowered to manage any part of the foundation's activities is considered to be acting on powers delegated to him by the board, which can be revoked at any time by dismissing and, possibly, replacing him.

Members of the board are bound by "proper business practice," and they are liable for any default on this practice or any breach of responsibility. They must act to the best of their knowledge and ability in their efforts to implement the settler's instructions concerning distribution of benefits. It is normally presumed that the board does not nominate beneficiaries. But one can give them this right, or, as is more common, designate beneficiaries on a group basis (e.g., "all my grandsons"), with the board specifying the individual beneficiaries. This power of designation becomes larger if the original specification is vague. Does one's "family" include an illegitimate son? The illegitimate daughter of the cousin of one's mother-in-law? If a settler were to be so unfortunately inexplicit as to what he meant by "family," and he is no longer around to ask, the board will have to decide to the best of its knowledge.

The board's primary responsibility is to the settler. But he can transfer to it his power of supreme authority, transfer it to someone else, or, simply, die. In the latter case, it is the public supervisory authorities of Liechtenstein and the foundation's beneficiaries to whom the board becomes responsible. If one so wishes, the terms of settlement may allow the beneficiaries to sue the board collectively, or its individual members, for not respecting the rights and benefits granted them by the terms of settlement. Similarly, anyone who can prove a legitimate interest in the foundation's property can lodge a complaint with the authorities against the board for failing to act on the settlement terms or for violating the purposes of the foundation.

A third foundation official that may but need not be appointed by the settler is a custodian. He can be given the power, say, of supervising payments of benefits as to amount, type, and recipients. Or he can be appointed to take care of the money due untraceable beneficiaries, in which case it is his duty to manage the money properly.

A fourth body, optimal for board supervision, is a body of auditors. They, too, are not legally required.

One can decide if such a body should exist, how its members are to be selected, what its range of responsibility should be, and so on.

Another optional body is that of collators. They can handle the function of nominating beneficiaries within the limited range the settler prescribes. They can also be empowered to implement the settler's general instructions concerning mode, time, and conditions of benefit payments. In this case, the board is left only with the duty of management and administration.

Of course, the more optional bodies employed, the greater the defense provided for the beneficiaries—and the larger the operating costs of the foundation. Thus, one's choice in these matters should balance up the risks to beneficiaries against the costs of maintenance.

There are some fixed statutory requirements a foundation board must satisfy: keeping normal accounts and issuing statements of liabilities and assets and of profits and losses on fixed specific dates. This duty can be transferred to an accountancy firm the board nominates. If one so decides, he can retain the power to inspect the accounts and to make decisions based on them. Alternatively, some independent party may supervise the board to guarantee due performance. Thus, the beneficiaries or any subgroup of them could be granted the right to audit the accounts and act on the basis of the audit.

A foundation can be revoked before registration (if such is necessary) or before documentation is completed, and if it is testamentary, any time before the settler's death. If the terms of settlement so specify, one can leave the right of revocation to himself, in the same way he can explicitly empower himself to modify the terms of settlement. The right of revocation can also be left to one or more heirs.

There is a legal distinction between the two basic types of revocation. A foundation revoked before full documentation or registration has taken place is revoked "on the grounds of insufficiency of intention" as a special case of "insufficiency of contract." This is known as revocation *ex tunc,* or retroactive revocation. It legally cancels the existence of the foundation before its inception. In this case, no claims can be made against the foundation; all liabilities incurred by it become the settler's personal liabilities.

The second type of revocation is that of a fully constituted foundation. This is known as *ex nunc* ("from now") revocation. All rights and liabilities incurred by the foundation are then valid, and it cannot properly be liquidated without full discharge, to the extent of its existing assets, of all liabilities. The only exception here is that in the terms of settlement one can provide for an automatic and immediate and even retroactive expiry of the benefits granted to beneficiaries.

Thus, a foundation can cease to exist because it is revoked by whoever has the right under its terms to revoke it. Of course, it can be liquidated once it has accumulated money for its perpetuity period, distributed all of it, and discharged all its debts. It can also be annulled by the government if the object of the foundation becomes unattainable or unworthy of pursuit (e.g., the beneficiaries have all died); if the foundation cannot act any more to achieve these aims due to insolvency; or if the terms of settlement are legally defective beyond cure. The state supervisory authorities impose and execute annulment, but have no further right to supervise or inspect in any way the day-to-day activities of the foundation unless the settler specifically grants them this right.

The concept of "beneficiary" is further refinable. One can separate *beneficiaries in law*—those granted the right to legally enforce on the board the benefits they are due—from the *beneficiaries in fact,* those not granted enforcement rights. Similarly, one can nominate *conditional beneficiaries,* those entitled to benefits only if certain conditions obtain as spelled out in the terms of settlement (e.g., other beneficiaries are dropped, a certain age is reached). Conditional beneficiaries have to agree in writing to accept the status of beneficiaries and, when the time comes, provide proper proof that whatever conditions were stipulated for benefits have been fulfilled. Unconditional beneficiaries are assumed to have agreed to receive benefits.

One can empower the board to revoke beneficiary status if certain conditions are fulfilled. But the board has to exercise this power within five years of the event that constitutes satisfaction of the condition. Alternatively, one can set as a condition that, say, a beneficiary must have no criminal record of a certain kind, in which case the time limitation does not apply.

As for oneself being a beneficiary, there can be circumstances under which a court may order a foundation to support the settler when it is proved that due to the establishment of the foundation he became incapable of paying his own debts. This implies, in effect, that one cannot abuse the foundation's status as a legal person and his power as supreme authority to establish a foundation from borrowed money, name himself sole beneficiary, and then declare bankruptcy.

If the mode of paying benefits is not specified, then they are assumed to be in cash. If they are supposed to amount to a specified fixed sum per year without specifying that this sum actually will be given each year, it is possible to discharge them in one lump payment that can be proved to be equal to the purchase of an annuity that would yield the specified annual sum.

Beneficiaries can go into court to defend their rights, as in a case where the board treats differently beneficiaries that are not differently treated in the terms of settlement. There is a legal presumption that equal benefits are to be given to all beneficiaries unless the settler has explicitly indicated otherwise. Also, the board cannot nominate beneficiaries if not explicitly given the right to do so, or if they have a closed list of beneficiaries, or if a body of collators exists for the purpose.

If no specification of either beneficiaries or of a way to nominate them exists, the settler and his legal heirs after him are legally assumed to be sole beneficiaries according to the following rules: If one's children are appointed beneficiaries, the law considers them all to be his issue otherwise entitled to be his heirs. If his spouse is nominated as beneficiary, his surviving wife is deemed legally to be beneficiary if she has not remarried. (Remember, this happens when one does not stipulate to the contrary.) When no beneficiaries have been nominated and the settler is dead, the Liechtensteinian inheritance law applying to heirs when there is no will would specify beneficiaries.

It is important to understand the way Liechtensteinian foundation law works as exemplified by the second rule. It is primarily a system of presumptions, not rigid restrictions. These presumptions apply when one does not specify something explicitly and do not apply when one's specific formulation excludes them. Where no presumptions exist, one must make a specification; otherwise, the foundation will be inoperative. For instance, one must spell out for each beneficiary (or for all of them as a group) whether or not benefit claims are to be made against the foundation investment returns or the original endowment. Otherwise, the board makes the decision, however arbitrarily.

To avoid the abuse of foundations there exist some statutory requirements that are inflexible. Among them is the rule that creditors take precedence over beneficiaries. A foundation cannot legally pay benefits and avoid paying debts. Creditors, naturally, have the right to sue the board for failing to comply with this requirement. Also, there exists a legal requirement that whoever is granted by the terms of settlement the power to dissolve the foundation also has the power to make a partial distribution to the beneficiaries and, thereby, reduce their rights.

It is easy to see that this system of presumptions and rules, combined with a settler's very wide powers and the fact that board powers are, essentially, residual, make the foundation much more flexible than corporations and trusts. One can reserve all powers and not be bound by the inflexible powers of a trustee or board of directors. Moreover, one can enjoy the "alter ego" of a legal entity without any public scrutiny such as that resulting from incorporation. A corporation must be registered; a foundation, like a trust, can be constituted with complete privacy and can operate with truly confidential, impenetrable numbered bank accounts.

As good as it is, the foundation is not the optimal Liechtensteinian profit-making entity. The prize in this category goes to the establishment.

Unlike the foundation, the establishment exists for economic purposes and not family or other "supporting" ends. It is a corporate body, with its own assets serving as sole backing for its own liabilities. It has its own internal organization and its own basic initial capital, allowing it to pursue lasting economic aims with no perpetuity period.

An establishment has a founder, similar to a foundation settler. The founder is a legal personality, not necessarily a physical one. He can be one's agent or attorney. He can also be the owner of a certificate on which there is no name, like a bearer share. The founder must sign the articles of incorporation, and his signature must be authenticated by a notary.

The articles of incorporation must specify:

Name of the Establishment. This can be any fancy designation that includes no national names or references to Liechtenstein or any sort of subtitle. It must include the word *Anstalt* ("establishment"), and it must not be misleading as to the nature of the foundation or immoral or illegal.

The name may include two parts, one of general

application, which can be used by many establishments simultaneously (such as "establishment for timber processing"), the other specific, original, or descriptive. This second part can be used only by the originating establishment, which thereby gains exclusive right to it.

The limitations on names implies, of course, that establishments, as against foundations and trusts, and like corporations, must be registered. It is up to the registrar to guarantee that the name satisfies all legal requirements and does not violate any prior right of use. Failure to register may incur serious penalties under the law.

Purpose of the Establishment. This can be, but need not be, private profit, as well as public utility. It can be stated narrowly or broadly. Any later change in purpose requires an amendment of the articles. Of course, the purpose must be both legal and moral; failing that, it is assumed that the establishment never existed as a legal person. If it becomes legally established, it has all the legal rights of a person to property, name, and honor (i.e., it can sue for libel and slander). Dissolution on the grounds of immoral or illegal purpose, however, is a *retroactive* annihilation of this status of legal personality. It requires the decision of an administrative tribunal following an administrative complaint or a trial. When such an unhappy event occurs, the court is empowered to suspend all the activities of the establishment, to confiscate all its property, and to use it to pay the establishment's creditors. Any remaining assets can be confiscated by the government.

Dissolution can also take place when the original goals of an establishment were not illegal or immoral but the establishment operates outside its allowed zone of activity as delimited by its articles. In this case, the state can take over the management of the establishment to pursue the original goals, and it can also, in the case of serious trouble, confiscate whatever remains of the establishment's property after debts have been paid.

Capitalization. There is a minimum paid-in capital requirement of 30,000 Swiss francs if there are no participation shares or associates' rights. Otherwise, the minimum is 50,000 Swiss francs. The appropriate minimum can, if cash, be proved by bank certificate. If the minimum is not met by a cash deposit in a bank but is in other forms, evidence of its assessed value by recognized competent assessors must be provided.

If participation shares are included, these can have a par value or represent a proportion of ownership. In the latter case, a specific, explicit statement to that effect must be included in the articles. Also, all shares must be fully paid-in, registered in a special ledger, and a specific body, as indicated in the articles, must be authorized to allow or disallow their transfer. All these complications can be avoided if the establishment has a single owner, the founder. Then he has the right to allocate profits as he likes, as well as the rights to change the articles when he sees fit, appoint and dismiss directors, etc. His legal heir inherits his founder's rights.

When ownership is divided among shareholders, founder's rights are conferred upon the general meeting of shareholders. Alternatively, the articles may specify that the board of directors inherits from the general meeting part or all of its powers. Again, it is assumed, unless specifically excluded by the articles, that only beneficiaries of the establishment are members of the general meeting and that they all have equal voting rights. But the articles may explicitly allow for nonbeneficiary founders with voting rights, or for unequal voting rights.

Organization. The articles must specify the operating organs of the establishment. The founder, as supreme authority, or alternatively, in the case of several founders and divided ownership, the general assembly, has already been discussed. Another indispensable organ is the board of directors. This can include any number of legal persons having the right to represent the establishment to third parties and sign contracts and commitments in its name, either individually, collectively, or in any combination provided by the articles. The assumption is that the term of appointment is three years, but the articles can specify any period and can allow for the firing and replacement of any director at any time by the supreme authority. There is a presumption that when the number of directors has been reduced by firing, resignation, or mortality, the board can continue business as usual with a reduced number.

There is one inflexible requirement: There must be at least one Liechtensteinian citizen resident director. He can, however, be a proxy supplied by a local representative. The names and addresses of all directors, managers, and those proxies allowed to sign for the company, must be entered in the government company register.

The board may act within the limits determined by the founder in the establishment articles and usually is assumed to have the right to hire employees for the establishment. The board is presumed, unless otherwise stated in the articles, to act collectively, and if individual directors are allowed to act individually under certain circumstances, the validity of such action is lost if objected to by another director. On the other hand, once the board signs a contract with the intention of binding the establishment, such legal binding exists, even if the establishment is not explicitly mentioned. The board is bound by standard business practice and responsible to the supreme authority. Its normal responsibilities include appointment and dismissal of staff, implementation of the founder's instructions, organization and expansion of the activities of the establishment within the limits set by the articles and by law, keeping complete accounts and records, and submission of annual reports to the supreme authority to permit it to reach independent conclusions.

Being a member of the board imposes certain duties on an individual. He cannot start a business competing with the establishment or be involved with one unless already so involved when he took his office, this fact being known to the establishment founder at the time. In this case, it is presumed that he is free of the normal obligation not to work for the competition by virtue of special permission from the founder. In case of violation of this conflict-of-interest principle, both immediate dismissal by the founder, without compensation, as well as a legal case for damages against the offending director is possible. It is possible, for instance, to demand that he transfer the advantages of a deal he made for himself to the establishment or give it whatever benefits he received from such a deal. But such action can be taken only within a year of discovery of the improper behavior of the offending board member.

The right to represent the company is transferable from the board to specific managers, each within the domain allocated to him as his responsibility by the board. The board's method of operation, meeting, reaching decisions, and signing in the name of the establishment has to be specified in the articles.

Methods of Accounting, Handling Balance Sheets, and Giving Notices to Relevant Parties. A body of auditors can be included in the organization, authorized to ascertain that the balance sheets, inventories, and profit and loss accounts agree with the books, that the books are properly kept, and that the information in them is accurate. It is their duty to report to the supreme authority (founder) any discrepancy or irregularity. Bookkeeping, annual balance sheets, annual statements of assets and liabilities, and copies of correspondence are required by law for all corporations and corporate-like business organizations, including establishments. The auditors may, additionally, represent the establishment to third parties unless they are explicitly denied this right in the articles. They can be appointed, for only one year at a time, and reappointed only twice, a maximum of three years altogether.

The articles must also comply with statutory requirements for giving notices. If the establishment deals locally, all communications must be published in the official gazette. If not, a legal representative (a Liechtensteinian citizen and resident) has to post them on a court notice board.

Provisions for Liquidation and Dissolution of the Establishment. These are restricted by law and must involve giving notice to creditors through a public notice in the publication organ specified in the articles. Within six months, if all liabilities have been duly discharged, the name of the establishment is struck off the books. If the liquidator finds out that liabilities exceed assets, all activities must be suspended and the courts informed about the bankruptcy. In the period of liquidation, the establishment is still a legal person, but the words "in liquidation" must be included in its name. Its liquidators gain the rights of directors and are bound with respect to the founder, his heirs, and creditors in the same way normal board members are, though they are exempted from the prohibition against working for competing firms or competing with the establishment that is imposed on board members.

Liquidation also involves its accounting counterpart. Liquidation balance sheets, indicating all liabilities discharged, debts paid, assets sold, and cancellation of registration effected must be submitted to the founder. During the period of liquidation, no dividends to shareholders are payable. The books of the liquidated establishment must be preserved for ten years, and anybody with valid claims after liquidation is completed will be granted permission to inspect them. Such claims become valid against the legal successors of the establishment, those who collected what was left of the assets after all preceding debts have been repaid.

An establishment must be registered by the state. Costs for this are as follows: formation duty of 2 percent of capital, registration fees of 100 Swiss francs for capital up to 100,000 Swiss francs, and variable stamp duties.

If an establishment trades locally, it must pay a capital tax of 0.2 percent of its capital and reserves plus a profits tax. The profits tax ranges from 5 percent to 12 percent, and within these limits the rate is one-half the ratio of the net profit to the total capital. For example, if the profits are 10 percent of capital, a 5 percent profits tax is due. If an establishment trades only outside Liechtenstein, its sole liability is a 0.1 percent annual capital tax. If ownership is divided into shares, 3 percent of dividends paid is taken as a coupon tax—another good reason to set up an establishment without shares.

The possibility of taxes because of either local involvement or divided ownership implies the general necessity of annual tax returns of profit and loss to show whether or not an establishment has any tax liabilities apart from the basic standard capital taxes. All these monies are official payments.

It is hard to establish general figures for annual maintenance and management because there are so many variables. Individual circumstances will dictate whether or not a Liechtensteinian establishment is worth setting up.

Apart from the foundation and the establishment, simple incorporation in Liechtenstein may offer benefits similar to those that can be obtained in other no-tax-on-foreign-income havens. These advantages should be considered carefully, since Liechtenstein offers Swiss-type bank facilities, monetary freedom, and privacy. On the other hand, one should bear in mind that a Liechtensteinian corporation is much more suspect in the eyes of tax authorities than, say, a Hong Kong corporation.

In Liechtenstein, ownership of a corporation can be divided not only into shares but into fractions, or quotas, and the relevant documents must specify the total sum of capital and reserves.

Division into fractions or quotas simply means that each certificate represents a percentage of the corporation instead of a fixed number of shares. For example, it may be for 10 percent of the capital, and would simply state on the certificate that it represents 10 percent ownership of the corporation. Shares can be without par value, and bearer shares are also allowed. The articles of incorporation can allow conversion of one kind of share to another, as well as for variable capital, within certain limits. The latter possibility requires the use of shares rather than certificates of ownership of fractions or quotas. Further, Liechtenstein allows the articles of incorporation to specify the proportion of bearer shares to be paid-in, subject to a legal minimum of 50 percent.

The articles of incorporation have to specify the usual things: corporate name and registered office address, capitalization (amount of initial capital, division into shares, nature of shares, nature and amount of paid-up capital, and the amount to be paid-up for each share), method of calling the general meeting of shareholders, governing bodies of the corporation and the manner in which members are appointed and dismissed to and from positions on them, and the form of communication of notices to shareholders and third parties.

Apart from these standard clauses, one could add

extra provisions that may relate to the value of non-cash contributions, special privileges of founding shareholders as against those who buy in later, and provisions relating to special amendments needed to general corporate law in its application to the particular corporation (e.g., how articles can be amended, how changes of authorized capital are to be executed, how mergers are to be performed). Additional restrictions, such as a built-in limitation on the life of the corporation, limits on the transfer of registered shares, differentiation in the voting power of certain kinds of shares, etc., can also be included.

An extra flexibility is offered by the fact that local law allows two forms of incorporation, so as to permit appeal to public finance in the process of formation itself. The first mode, "simultaneous" incorporation, involves the standard procedures. The founders sign a memorandum declaring incorporation of the company, sanction the articles, confirm their acceptance of all shares, and pay for them.

The second mode, "successive" incorporation is unique to Liechtenstein. Here the founders need not subscribe to all shares, but merely to some of them. They lay down and sign the articles, subscribe to their part of the share issue, and offer the remaining shares to the public. After all shares have been subscribed to, a general meeting of all shareholders is convened to decide on the appointment of officers and the confirmation of the articles. Successive incorporation requires a prospectus specifying all relevant details concerning the articles, times for subscription and payment, subscription offices, the issue price of shares, and how much has to be paid-in before the first general meeting of shareholders.

Under either method, incorporation requires a minimum paid-in capital of 50,000 Swiss francs. Registered shares can be subscribed to by a mere 20 percent premium, as against the already mentioned 50 percent premium on bearer shares. As usual, the difference between the issue price of a share and the premium is a liability of the shareholder to the corporation.

In an instance in which the paid-in capital includes noncash assets, or in which some shareholders are granted certain special privileges by the articles, the founders must publish a written report setting forth the cash value of the noncash contributions and/or why privileges have been granted. These reports must be open to public inspection in any subscription office, because when an individual subscribes he is entitled to know why other shareholders will have privileges he will not have, what they are, and how noncash payments are valued. Moreover, any group of shareholders controlling 10 percent of the shares is entitled to enforce expert evaluation of the noncash assets as well as independent evaluation of any special privileges. If this right is invoked, both reports would be discussed in the next general shareholders' meeting, and if they are rejected by majority vote, the shareholders are entitled to a refund. Any such peculiarities as noncash contributions and special privileges to special shareholders require the approval of three-fourths of the shareholders.

Only when this sequential process is completed, all shares subscribed, all special features are approved, and officers appointed, is registration in the commercial register effected. Registration cannot be accomplished unless the minimum paid-in capital of 50,000 Swiss francs is fully certified by bank documents or assessment of noncash contributions or both.

Sequential incorporation allows one to solicit strangers to participate in a corporation. Another possibility for financing comes from the right Liechtensteinian companies have to float bonds to shareholders and the general public. Bonds may entitle their owner to the right to buy future shares when issued, but they do not carry voting rights.

While Liechtensteinian corporations are flexible, the flexibility has its own built-in restrictions. Variable capital is allowed, but it is only allowed with registered shares. Increasing capital requires selling more shares. Decreasing capital requires buying up shares and canceling them. The maximum capital cannot be more than ten times the minimum, as specified in the articles, and must be specified as well. Any act of purchasing and canceling shares requires a liquidation balance sheet showing that after repayment the liabilities of the corporation are still covered by its remaining assets, reserves, and capital. The specific mode of buying shares back must be set forth in the articles.

Another possibility for handling repurchased shares is to "freeze" them for awhile and resell them later. Since such "frozen" shares have neither voting nor dividend rights, this is equivalent to canceling and reissuing the same shares—within the limits of variability of capital allowed by the articles. Another restriction is that if the minimum authorized capital of the corporation is higher than the legal minimum of paid-in capital (more than 50,000 francs), there is a statutory requirement of a yearly accumulation of 10 percent of net profits in a reserve fund until the minimum is reached. This 10 percent is, therefore, not distributable as dividends.

Liechtensteinian corporations can be liquidated in a number of ways: by court action due to illegal or immoral operations or bankruptcy; in accordance with specifications in the articles; and by a majority vote to liquidate in a general shareholders' meeting.

A corporation must keep books, and its board must submit annual balance sheets to the general meeting within six months of the end of the accounting year. For a corporation with more than one million Swiss francs' capitalization and for any corporation with bonds outstanding, balance sheets and profit and loss accounts must be publicly published.

Apart from the minimum capitalization requirement, the cost of incorporation depends on the capital involved: 200 Swiss francs on the first 100,000 Swiss francs and a further 50 Swiss francs for each additional 100,000 Swiss francs or fraction thereof. On top of this, there are small stamp duties and certification costs.

As for maintenance, there is an annual capital tax of 0.1 percent of the total capital (with a minimum tax of 1,000 Swiss francs). If a company is either a holding company or a domiciliary company—that is, if it specializes in holding investment portfolios or if it operates only outside Liechtenstein—no further taxes apply. Local operations, however, involve some additional taxes. There is an earnings tax of 1–5 percent if annual dividends total more than 24 percent of taxable capital, and the capital tax is 0.2 percent. All companies, including domiciliatory and holding companies, pay a 3 percent coupon tax on dividends and a 3 percent tax on interest paid to bondholders. And every company must annually file with the government a balance sheet, a profit and loss account, and details concerning the coupon tax. Of course, to these taxes must be added the expenses associated with paying board members, company officers, and so on.

Liechtenstein is outstanding among civil law countries when it comes to trusts. It is an exception to the rule that civil law nations either do not allow trusts or, if they do, the trusts they allow are less than desirable.

In Liechtenstein, trust law considers a trust to be a contract between the trustor and the trustee. It is a private contract that does not require registration with a public registrar and is thus a very private affair. The trust property is whatever estate, funds, or other property one allocates to the trust, and it can be described in the trust instruments in as great or as little detail as one might like. It contains, of course, the principal plus accumulated revenue of investment returns and/or compensation for damages incurred to property. The trust, in view of its private nature, is *not* a separate legal entity, and does not have limited liability. The trustee is personally or corporatively liable for debts (not including taxes) incurred by the trust property he manages, and he has the right of legal recourse against both the trustor and the beneficiaries, unless the trust instrument explicitly excludes this right.

The trust property is managed, legally, under the title of the trustee, in accordance with his appointment by the trustor. The trustee is entitled to a salary for his services and reimbursement of all expenses incurred by him in managing the trust and for damages that might be incurred by his property by the trust property.

An advantage of Liechtensteinian trusts is that they can operate under the laws of, say, the Cayman Islands or Hong Kong, to be applied locally by Liechtensteinian courts. The major drawback is the fact that the trust is not a legal person, and thus its income is taxed to the trustor. To avert this, another special Liechtensteinian entity exists: the trust enterprise.

The trust enterprise is a legal person, managed by a trustee. It must be registered in the commercial registry as a "registered trust." This is in line with the fact that legal entities can *usually* be formed only through the state. Private agreements usually cannot create legal entities (Liechtensteinian foundations excluded).

The corporate document of the trust enterprise, the trust statement, must specify all that is usual for corporations: the name of the trust, the registered office address, the perpetuity period (not limited by law), the purposes and objects of the trust enterprise, and a statement of limited liability. Apart from the trust statement, trust articles are needed, specifying the amount and nature of funds (with a separate list of items), the number of trustees and the method of appointing and replacing them.

The minimum capital required of a trust enterprise is 30,000 Swiss francs, fully paid-in, though not necessarily all in cash. As against common law trusts, the purpose of a trust enterprise can be business, family support, or philanthropy. The trustees are legally free to make investment decisions in accordance with whatever provisions are specified in the trust articles. Their expenses and salaries are paid out of the trust enterprise's revenues unless the articles otherwise specify. The trust enterprise, being a legal personality, covers its liabilities through its assets alone. The trustor, trustee(s), and beneficiaries become legally liable only due to some violation of the trust articles or through illegal exploitation of the trust.

Trust entities are taxed like other corporate entities in Liechtenstein. If all income comes from abroad, a mere 0.1 percent annual capital tax is due. Local activities are penalized by the local taxes mentioned above. Finally, trust enterprises, like private trusts, can be made subject to any other country's laws, with local courts applying them.

The great flexibility of Liechtensteinian corporate and trust laws, the various tax advantages, the absolute privacy available, the monetary freedom, and the soundness of the Swiss franc together explain why 20,000 companies are registered in Liechtenstein. Since each of them pays the government a minimum of 1,000 Swiss francs a year, this adds up to very important revenues for a country with but 20,000 citizens. It is unlikely, to say the least, that this paradise for wise investors will go aglimmering any time soon!

ELEVEN

Switzerland: Less than Meets the Eye

The reader may have wondered why Switzerland and Liechtenstein are not considered together in a chapter on European havens. The reason is simple: Switzerland is *not* a tax haven. Not any more.

This may come as a shock. Many people think "tax haven" means a numbered account with a Swiss bank. This is a fallacy today. Switzerland is no longer even a banking haven, and all its remaining advantages are offered by Hong Kong, Liechtenstein, and other countries without its present disadvantages. Such a conclusion is liable to be greeted with considerable skepticism. So let us detail why Switzerland is not a tax haven and why those seeking a haven should stay out of the Swiss Alps.

Why is Switzerland so widely considered a tax haven? To begin with, there is its remarkable internal and international political stability. It has been a most successfully neutral country in many European wars and both world wars, so in modern times, its economy has never been devastated by war's destruction. Also, it is a basically free enterprise country with little government regulation and economic control and relatively low taxes. Its banks have had a tradition of inviolate secrecy, stability, and reliability. Its currency, the Swiss franc, has a very good reputation and is very strong and stable.

The country is geographically in the center of Europe, where major continental roads from east, west, north, and south intersect. Its internal roads and railways are excellent, and all its transportation services are punctual. It is also accessible by river barge directly from the sea. Airline service is tops, and telecommunications are the very best available. Needless to say, professional services are of the very highest quality and reliability.

As we have noted, Switzerland is politically stable, as is well attested to by its history, legal structure, and present socioeconomic situation. Its basic constitution, enacted in 1848 and slightly revised in 1974, gives the country a confederation system. It has 123 articles, specifying rights and duties of both citizens and the government. The twenty-five cantons (states) have inalienable constitutional rights that cannot be usurped by the federal government. There is a seven-man national cabinet, nationally elected. The foreign policy has for centuries been peaceful neutrality concerning all international conflicts. The legal system is grounded in the civil law tradition.

Switzerland is multilingual; German, French, Italian, and Romansch are official languages. German is the most widespread tongue, having a variety of local dialects. English and French are universally taught in the high schools, and the business community is widely conversant with them.

Switzerland is known for its free-exchange market in currencies. In the past, one could deposit whatever currency he liked in Swiss banks, convert it locally to Swiss francs, and preserve the value of his money against inflation. Since 1972, however, a negative interest of 2 percent per quarter has been imposed on large Swiss franc deposits of foreigners, reducing one's deposit in a fashion similar to inflation.

Both the federal government and the cantons as well as the municipalities tax separately, with cantonal taxes the heaviest. Companies are taxed both on their profits and on their capital by the federal government and the cantons, as well as the "community."

Company taxes are not flat but progressive. The brackets depend not on the total volume of a company's profits, but as in Liechtenstein, on the "profit intensity," the ratio of profits to capital. The intensity is divided by two to derive the federal tax rate, within a range of 2.25–7.6 percent. All taxes on worldwide income add up to 25–35 percent. Thus, one could probably do business in Switzerland with lower taxes than in the United States, but Switzerland is clearly no tax haven. There is a double-taxation agreement with the U.S., reducing the U.S. withholding tax to 15 percent. However, when this is combined with local taxes on what remains, a total tax of about 40 percent has been paid! The individual income tax is also progressive and is levied on the total of one's worldwide income.

There is special tax treatment for holding companies. This special treatment applies also to ordinary companies to the extent that they operate as holding companies and derive income from merely "passive" sources (dividends, interest, etc.). Such tax exemptions are highly limited, however; for instance, they do not apply to interest from loans and royalties from leases paid by companies in which one has stock ownership. Still, a pure holding company pays no federal income tax, only a federal capital tax of 0.0825 percent of the value of share capital and a similar canton capital tax.

Domiciliatory companies, those based in Switzerland but doing business only outside the country, have been granted exemptions from local income taxes by some cantons. The applicable taxes are reduced cantonal capital tax, federal income tax, and federal capital tax.

Apart from these taxes, one has to consider a turnover tax of 4–5 percent against payment on the internal delivery of goods by a wholesaler. This can be avoided if the goods are immediately exported or if they are merely in transit. There is a similar tax on imported goods, on top of the import duty.

Even with a purely investment-holding company, there is one huge liability: a 35 percent withholding tax imposed on dividends paid to foreign stockholders. It applies indiscriminately to dividends, interest on bonds, and interest on bank deposits; only royalties are exempted.

Might not the double-taxation agreement between the United States and Switzerland allow one to consider Switzerland as a base for a holding company? On the surface, this seems to be so. The agreement reduces the U.S. withholding tax on dividends to 15 percent. However, the Swiss government has taken special measures to restrict the usability of the agreement for tax minimization purposes. If, say, more than 50 percent of the profits of a Swiss company derived from U.S. sources are paid to aliens, no withholding tax benefits can be claimed. One may think that the way out is not to distribute to himself dividends from his Swiss company and instead reinvest all profits. However, another law requires a company to pay as dividends at least 25 percent of the gross income derived from tax-relief benefits. Thus, there are narrow limits to using the agreement.

On top of these disadvantages, Swiss incorporation is expensive. There is a stamp duty of 2 percent on authorized capital.

If all this is not enough, neither the joint stock company nor the private limited liability company, the two business entities available in Switzerland, offers any particular tax advantages.

"Well," one might think, "what about those numbered accounts?" Many people believe that, while Swiss business entities are costly, unprivate, and very restrictive, a numbered account may offer a defense against taxes and inflation. Unfortunately, this is not so. We have already mentioned the negative interest of 2 percent per quarter on Swiss franc accounts of foreigners. Add to this a recent American-Swiss agreement to penetrate the veil of secrecy of numbered accounts and to require banks to reveal information about an account holder if the U.S. authorities demand it on the claim that the owner, or alleged owner, is suspected of being involved in organized crime. Such claims can be made and are hard to disprove, either in the United States or Switzerland. If the IRS suspects that someone is evading taxes on a large sum possibly deposited in Switzerland, it can have the Justice Department ask the Swiss for information on whether or not the "suspect" has such an account, and the account probably will be disclosed.

All in all, as a tax haven, Switzerland is a good place for a vacation. Go there, enjoy the skiing and the bracing air, but put your investments elsewhere.

Epilogue

The purpose of this book has been to bring to the reader's attention the vast array of advantages available in tax havens for shrewd investors who are seriously interested in minimizing their tax burdens. How these advantages may be put to use is up to the individual, and the possible approaches are very nearly as many as the number of people who will read these words.

It has not been my intention to recommend any particular course of action. To do so without personal consultation and very careful consideration of individual circumstances would be irresponsible and ineffective. The only way an intelligent investor can make sound decisions on putting tax havens to work for himself is by consulting expert tax advisors, considering carefully all the ins and outs, and then and only then choosing and carrying out a careful program.

I am the president of a consulting firm specializing in tax havens and overseas banking and finance.

Readers who are interested in pursuing a tax haven investment program are invited to write:

Minerva Consulting Group, Inc.
200 Park Avenue
New York, NY 10017

APPENDIX

Tax Haven Facts and Figures

The Bahamas Islands

Coordinate Location. 22N, 75W.

Geographic Location. The island chain begins about fifty miles southeast of Miami, Florida, and lies in a southeasterly direction in the Atlantic Ocean.

Topography. The Bahamas consist of fourteen large islands, with numerous small islands and cays, many of which are uninhabited. The terrain is low-lying and flat, with mangrove swamps, lakes and ponds. The highest elevation is about 400 feet above sea level.

Area. The area of the Bahamas is about 5,382 square miles.

Climate. The winter temperature of the Bahamas averages about seventy-two degrees, and the average summer temperature is about eighty-four degrees. There is an average annual rainfall of forty-six inches, falling mostly in the summer. There is occasional hurricane activity.

Capital City. Nassau.

Population. About 200,000.

Ethnic Makeup. The population is a mixture of European and African, the latter being the result of early slave trade. About 85 percent of the population is black. There has been an influx of British and U.S. residents.

Language. The official language of the Bahamas is English.

Currency. The official currency of the Bahamas is the Bahamian dollar (B$), which equals one dollar, U.S.

Transportation. There is no railway system in the Bahamas. There are about 600 miles of highways, suitable for passenger cars, trucks and buses, about one-half of which are paved. There are about forty-six airports, with varying accommodations, most of which serve interisland aircraft. There are international airports at Nassau, Freeport and West End.

Communication. There are three daily newspapers: The *Nassau Guardian,* the *Nassau Tribune,* and the *Freeport News.* There are some government-operated radio stations. There is a telephone system, with efficient telephone communications to the U.S.

Living Accommodations. On a local level, there is a housing shortage, but executive level housing is usually available.

Education. There are over 200 primary schools (ages five to eleven). There are approximately 160 secondary schools (ages eleven to nineteen). There are some schools of higher education. The literacy rate is over 90 percent.

Religion. There are both Protestant and Catholic churches in the Bahamas.

Medical. Hospital and medical facilities are available.

Recreation and Culture. The islands are undergoing a revival of Island folk lore, with presentations by amateur choral, dramatic and dancing groups.

Government. The Bahamas is self-governing, having obtained independence from Great Britain in 1973. The government is patterned after that of Great Britain.

Political/Social Stability. Political and social unrest in the Bahamas is not unknown in the past; however, the current situation seems to pose no threat to foreign business there.

Barbados

Coordinate Location. 13N, 59W.

Geographic Location. The island of Barbados is one of the easternmost of the West Indies, situated in the Atlantic Ocean in the island chain called the Lesser Antilles, which separates the Atlantic from the Caribbean Sea, some 200 miles in a northerly direction from the north-facing coast of Venezuela.

Topography. Barbados is almost completely surrounded by coral reefs. The highest point of the island itself is Mt. Hillaby, reaching an elevation of 1,115 feet above the sea.

Area. 166 square miles.

Capital City. Bridgetown.

Population. About 250,000 (Barbados has the reputation of being one of the most densely populated countries in the world).

Language. The official language of Barbados is English.

Ethnic Makeup. Predominately Negro.

Currency. Barbados dollar.

Education. There are educational facilities in Barbados, and the literacy rate is high.

Religion. Due to the strong British influence in Barbados, the Anglican religion predominates.

Economy. The sustaining industries of Barbados are agriculture, tourism, lime quarrying, and the commercialization of flying fish. Local unemployment is high.

Government. Barbados is internally self-governing, with a governor-general, prime minister, and parliament.

Political Stability. Good.

Bermuda

Coordinate Location. 32N, 65.7W.

Geographic Location. Bermuda is located in the Atlantic Ocean, 570 miles east by southeast of Cape Hatteras, North Carolina.

Topography. The terrain is generally hilly, with fertile depressions. Flora is abundant, with about 950 kinds of flowering plants and trees. There are no rivers or lakes. The highest elevation is about 260 feet above sea level.

Area. 20.41 square miles.

Climate. The climate of Bermuda is mild, humid and frost-free. In August, the hottest month of the year, the temperature will average ninety degrees; in February, the coldest month, the average annual low temperature is forty-seven degrees.

Capital City. Hamilton.

Population. 52,700.

Ethnic Makeup. About 60 percent of Bermuda's population is black, with the remaining population a mixture of British, European, American and Canadian.

Language. The official language of Bermuda is English.

Currency. The Bermuda dollar (Ber$), which equals one dollar, U.S.

Transportation. There is no railway system in Bermuda. There are approximately 400 miles of highways to accommodate passenger cars, trucks, and buses. There is one airport with regularly scheduled flights.

Communications. There is a telephone system, operated by the Bermuda Telephone Co., Ltd. There are four radio stations, two television stations, one daily and three weekly newspapers.

Education. There are over thirty primary schools for ages five to twelve; about fifteen secondary schools for ages twelve to sixteen; and there are some vocational schools. The literacy rate is 100 percent. There are library and library branches.

Religion. Religion is represented in Bermuda by the Church of England, the African Methodist Episcopal and the Roman Catholic Church.

Medical. There are one general hospital and three specialized hospitals.

Recreation and Culture. Culture in Bermuda is represented by art, drama, choral singing, and several movie theaters. African folklore is kept alive by the Gombey Dancers. Kite flying is an island sport.

Government. Bermuda is a British colony with a system of self-government, with Britain retaining control of defense, foreign affairs, and the police. The elected leader of the majority party, together with a six-member executive council, advises a royally-appointed governor. There is a two-party system.

Political/Social Stability. There was political unrest in Bermuda in 1968. As recently as 1973, the governor, Sir Richard Sharples, was shot, following an earlier assassination of the police commissioner; and in 1977, when the murderers were hanged, major riots occurred. At this time, however, it appears that political tensions are not a major problem, and Bermuda boasts almost complete racial integration.

The British Virgin Islands

Coordinate Location. 18.5N, 64.5W.

Geographic Location. The British Virgin Islands lie directly east of Puerto Rico, and comprise a British territory in the larger group known as the Virgin Islands; the remaining islands in the group are U.S. controlled, and are called the U.S. Virgin Islands. The British group consists of four larger and about thirty-two smaller islands. The larger island of Tortola is the capital site. The other larger islands are Anegada, Virgin Gorda, and Jost Van Dyke.

Topography. Geologically, the islands are the peaks of submerged mountains that rise from a suboceanic plateau. Most of the islands rise to only a few hundred feet, with a few that rise to over 1,000 feet above sea level. The landscape varies from craggy cliffs and mountain peaks to small lagoons with coral reefs and barrier beaches; from level terrain to elevated plateaus with rolling land and jungle areas.

Climate. Except for rare hurricanes, the climate of the islands is considered ideal. Trade winds from the southwest cool the islands, and the humidity is low, with a negligible pollen count. The temperature never rises above ninety-six or falls below sixty-three at sea level, with an annual average of about seventy-eight degrees. A dry season occurs from February to July, a wet season from September to December; the average annual rainfall is forty inches. Hurricanes, when they occur, come between August and October. (The comparatively light rainfall, together with an inadequate natural storage for water necessitates rain catchments on the Islands to aid in the storage of a water supply.)

Capital City. Road Town (Island of Tortola).

Population. About 11,000.

Ethnic Makeup. Predominately of African descent, with a small percentage of whites, including American and British.

Language. The traditional language is English.

Currency. U.S. dollar.

Transportation. On the island of Tortola, two main highways and numerous side roads comprise forty miles of road; on Anageda there are thirty miles; new roads are under construction on Virgin Gorda and Jost Van Dyke.

Communications. A weekly newspaper, the *Island Sun,* is published in Road Town. There are radio stations and television service. The internal telephone system of the BVI is operated by Cable and Wireless, which also operates a reliable external cable, telex and radio-telephone service to all other parts of the world. There are direct telecommunications links with the U.S., Canada, and the United Kingdom; and island telephones can be direct-dialed from the U.S.

Education. There are approximately fifteen primary and secondary schools, no institutions of higher learning. There is a library in Road Town, with branches in the outlying British islands.

Religion. The religious affiliation in the islands is predominately Protestant; approximately 73 percent of the British Islanders are Methodist, and about 16 percent are Anglicans.

Government. A crown-appointed administrator is responsible for defense, internal security, external affairs, public service, courts and finance. The territory's law is derived from both the English common law and locally enacted laws.

Political Stability. Because of the small population, the islands are quite stable and likely to remain so. The problems of the U.S. Virgin Islands have not spilled over to the British islands.

The Cayman Islands

Coordinate Location. 19.5N, 80.5W.

Geographic Location. The Cayman Islands are located in the Caribbean Sea, 150 miles northwest of Jamaica, and south of Cuba.

Topography. The land is lowlying. Sections of the coast are reefed and rocky. There are no rivers.

Area. 118 square miles.

Climate. The average annual rainfall is 56 inches at the capital. The islands are in the hurricane area, with some hurricane damage having been recorded in the past.

Capital City. Georgetown.

Population. About 15,000.

Ethnic Makeup. The ethnic makeup of the Cayman population is mixed African-European descent. There are also English, American and other nationalities residing in the Caymans.

Language. English.

Currency. The Caymans currency is the Cayman Islands dollar, worth approximately $1.20, U.S.

Transportation. The Owens Roberts International Airport is located at Grand Cayman. It is capable of servicing medium-sized jets, and further improvements are being undertaken. There are two daily flights to Jamaica and Costa Rica. Flight time from Miami, Florida, is fifty minutes.

Communications. To provide communications, there are airmail, telephone, and telex systems, which are satisfactory and being improved. International communications is through a direct undersea cable, which links Georgetown, Grand Cayman, to the earth satellite station in Jamaica.

Government. The Caymans are a British colony, governed by an administrator and executive council, and a partially elected legislative assembly.

Political Stability. Political stability in the Caymans is good.

Costa Rica

Coordinate Location. 10N, 84W.

Geographic Location. Costa Rica is in Central America, bordering Nicaragua, which lies to the north, and Panama, which lies to the south. Its western coast is on the Pacific Ocean; its eastern coast is on the Caribbean Sea.

Topography. The terrain of Costa Rica varies from an inland plateau, which reaches an elevation of about 4,000 feet, to the lowlands of the coastal areas.

Area. 19,653 square miles.

Climate. The interior plateau of Costa Rica enjoys a temperate climate, changing to tropical in the lowlands.

Capital City. San José.

Population. About 2,000,000.

Language. The predominate language is Spanish, but English is taught in the schools.

Currency. The colon.

Economics. Costa Rica is primarily an agricultural nation, depending heavily upon the export of coffee, bananas, sugar, cocoa, cotton, and other agricultural products. Due largely to tax haven legislation, an influx of industries—such as the manufacture of fiberglass, aluminum, textiles, fertilizer, etc.—has created an industrial base in the country. There is also some mining and lumbering. The standard of living is good, and social services are available.

Transportation. A railway system connects the capital city of San José to the Caribbean port city of Puerto Limon; and to the port city of Puntarenas on the Pacific. There is also a good system of roads for trucks, buses and cars.

Education. Primary education is compulsory in Costa Rica, and higher education is free. The literacy rate is about 87 percent. There are universities in Cartago, Heredia, San José, and Turrialba.

Religion. Roman Catholicism predominates as the religion of Costa Rica.

Medical. Facilities are generally quite good.

Government. Costa Rica was once a part of the Confederation of Centralmerica, but it is now independent. A new constitution was adopted in 1949, which, among other acts, abolished the army as a permanent institution. A president, who is elected for four years, may not be reelected. Costa Rica citizens may be fined for not voting.

Political Stability. Costa Rica is politically stable.

Hong Kong

Coordinate Location. 25.2N, 114.2E.

Geographic Location. Situated in the South China Sea, Hong Kong comprises the island of Hong Kong and the adjacent mainland bordering China.

Topography. Geologically, Hong Kong is a drowned mountain range with hills that rise directly out of the sea, with cliffs and sea caves along the coastal areas. There are no coastal flats, but numerous mountain peaks, some of which rise to elevations of over 3,000 feet.

Area. 404 square miles.

Climate. Located at the northern limits of the tropical zone, Hong Kong has hot, humid summers and cool, dry winters; the mean average temperature in January is sixty degrees, and the mean average July temperature is eighty-two degrees. The average annual rainfall is eighty-five inches, with most of it occurring between April and October, occasionally in torrents. There is typhoon activity between July and October, and sometimes in November.

Capital City. Victoria.

Population. About 4,000,000.

Ethnic Makeup. Hong Kong is over 90 percent Chinese, about one-half of whom were born in Hong Kong. The remainder of the population is a variety of nationalities, predominately British and American, who are there primarily for business reasons.

Language. Chinese predominates, at least among the local Chinese. As in China, a variety of linguistic groups are represented in Hong Kong. English is the language of business and government.

Currency. Hong Kong dollar.

Transportation. Hong Kong boasts a railway system. There are a total of over 600 miles of roads in the colony, divided between Hong Kong Island, Kowloon, and New Territories. Major international airlines are serviced by Hong Kong airports.

Communications. There are over sixty daily newspapers, only four of which are printed in English. There is a broadcast station. There is approximately one phone for every 6.8 persons.

Living Accommodations. There is a critical housing shortage on a local basis, but there are hotel accommodations for visitors and businessmen on short-term stays.

Education. Education is modeled on the British system, with well over a million students attending schools at all levels; there are universities, but many students seek higher education in the U.S.

Religion. On a national level, Christianity is poorly represented, with Buddhism and Taoism predominating.

Medical. The government operates over a dozen general hospitals, and promotes health programs. Medical service is inexpensive, but not free.

Government. A governor, appointed by the British Crown, is the Queen's representative, and head of the executive branch of the colony. There is Chinese representation in the government.

Recreation. There are more than 100 movie theaters. Radio and television stations provide programming for the area.

Political Stability. Hong Kong is a thriving industrial community, with a viable economy and political stability. It appears that any threat that might have been posed by the nearness of Communist China is removed with the establishment of diplomatic relations between China and the U.S.

Liberia

Coordinate Location. 6N, 10E.
Geographic Location. On the west coast of Africa.

Topography. The topography is complex, varying from swamps to hilly country and mountains; Mt. Nimba rises to 4,500 feet. There are five major rivers.

Area. 43,000 square miles.

Climate. The coastal area of Liberia is warm and humid all year around. The rainfall is seasonal, occurring from May to October, followed by a dry season from November to April. Rainfall varies from an annual average of 205 inches on the Cape Mount promontory, to 70 inches on the central plateau area. In the dry season, the interior has hot but pleasant days and cool nights.

Capital City. Monrovia.

Population. Approximately 1,500,000.

Ethnic Makeup. Except for Europeans, British and Americans there for reasons of business, the population is primarily African, which can be broken down to three indigenous African tribes; and Negroes from the New World, called Americo-Liberians.

Language. Three linguistic tribal groups—the Mande, the Kru, and the Atlantic—predominate. English is the official language of government and business.

Currency. United States dollars are used, with Liberian coins.

Transportation. There are approximately 42,000 miles of roads, of which, approximately 325 miles are paved. The Liberian National Airways and Roberts International Airport are used by about twelve airlines. In 1968, in agreement with Liberian authorities, the Pan-American Airways took over the

management of all Liberian airfields. Several seaports serve the 350-mile coastline.
Political Stability. Good.

Liechtenstein

Coordinate Location. 47.4N, 8.5E.
Geographic Location. In Central Europe between Switzerland and Austria.
Topography. The eastern two-thirds of the country is made up of rugged foothills, which are a part of the Alps. Mountains rise 5,900–8,600 feet, with snow-covered peaks. The lower slopes are covered by Alpine flowers. The western section of the country is predominated by the Rhine River flood plain.
Climate. A mild climate is influenced by southerly winds called *foehn*. The annual combined total of rain and snow is from thirty-six to forty-five inches.
Capital City. Vaduz.
Population. Approximately 22,000.
Ethnic Makeup. The population is descended from the Alemanni tribe (Germanic in origin), and from the Walsers from the Swiss canton of Valais.
Language. German and Alemanni dialect with local variation in pronunciation and vocabulary.
Currency. The Swiss franc.
Transportation. Liechtenstein is served by the Austrian railway. There is a system of roads to accommodate the several thousands of passenger cars, buses, and trucks. There are excellent roads connecting the principality to its neighbors, Austria and Switzerland. There is no local airport.

Communications. There is one daily newspaper. There is radio and television reception, and a telephone system.

Education. The Liechtenstein school system has eight-year primary schools, three-year secondary schools, vocational schools, eight-year grammar schools, five-year commercial high schools, a school of music, a technical college, and a five-year commercial high school for girls. Everyone over the age of seven is literate. There is a national library.

Religion. The religion of Liechtenstein is 90 percent Roman Catholic. The remainder is Protestant.

Medical. One small hospital is supplemented by excellent medical facilities in neighboring Switzerland.

Recreation and Culture. Culturally, Liechtenstein encourages art by Liechtenstein artists. World-famous art collections are displayed in the Liechtenstein National Museum at Vaduz. The country is scenic and abounding in wildlife.

Government. Liechtenstein is a constitutional principality, in which the government's power derives from both the prince and the populace. The constitution provides for a fifteen-member parliament, elected to four-year terms. There are a chief, and a deputy-chief of government, and three councilors who are appointed to four-year terms.

Political Stability. Excellent.

Netherlands Antilles

Coordinate Location. The southernmost group of the Netherlands Antilles is located at 12.2N, 69W.

Geographic Location. The entire Netherlands Antilles consist of two widely separated island groups, one group being in the Leeward Islands, east by southeast of Puerto Rico, and the other just 60 miles off the coast of Venezuela; the group here discussed is the latter.

Area. The total area of both island groups is 385 square miles.

Capital City. Willemstad, on the island of Curacao.

Government. The Netherlands Antilles is an integral part of the Kingdom of the Netherlands (Holland). Executive authority is vested in the governor, appointed by the crown, and a seven-member council of ministers who are responsible to a legislature.

Political Stability. Good.

New Hebrides

Coordinate Location 16.3S, 167.7E.

Geographic Location. The New Hebrides is in the South Pacific Ocean, lying 1,100 miles east of Australia, 500 miles west of the Fiji Islands, and southeast of New Guinea. The islands of the New Hebrides group consist of a chain of 12 principal islands and numerous smaller islands.

Topography. The topography is varied, from rugged mountains and high plateaus to rolling hills and low plateaus, with coastal terraces and offshore coral reefs. Mt. Tabsenasana is the highest point in the islands, reaching an elevation of 6,195 feet. All the islands are forested.

Area. The total area of all the islands of the New Hebrides is 5,700 square miles.

Climate. The climate is subtropical, with the seasons reversed to those of our northern hemisphere.

Capital City. Vila.

Population. 86,000.

Ethnic Makeup. The ethnic makeup of the New Hebrides is Melanesian (oceanic negroid), with a multiracial community of Europeans, Chinese, Vietnamese, Tahitians, Wallis Islanders, and New Caledonians.

Language. The Melanesians, who are indigenous to the islands, speak Melanesian. Other predominate languages are English and French. Much of the linguistic mixing and civilization of the New Hebrides has come about as a result of the islands' role in World War II.

Currency. The Australian dollar is most commonly used.

Transportation. The shipping and airlines transportation system is geared to move goods in and out of the Pacific islands. Moderately fast and efficient transportation, in some form, is generally available between the islands of the New Hebrides and most of the major countries of the Pacific.

Communications. An extensive communications system has been developed in the New Hebrides, and it is under improvement. There are communications by radio, radio-telephone, and cable; and news services are available to the islands. Local broadcasts are given in English, French, Pidgin English, and in indigenous tongues.

Education. Near Vila there are education facilities, including a teachers' training college.

Medical. There are hospitals and clinics on the islands. The major health problem of the New Hebrides is malaria.

Government. In 1887, conflicting British and French interests were resolved by the establishment of a joint naval commission to administer the islands. By 1906 the two nations had agreed to exercise joint sovereignty over the indigenous peoples, with each nation being responsible for its own nationals. The New Hebrides is still jointly ruled by these two nations.

Political Stability. Recent developments in the New Hebrides, which are rooted in racial unrest, suggest that the prudent businessman should check on the current situation before making any decisions.

Panama

Coordinate Location. Approximately 9N, 79W.

Geographic Location. Geographically, Panama comprises a large area in Central America, and is the final connecting link of land between Central and South America.

Topography. There are three distinct topographical sections in Panama: the lowlands, below 2,300 feet in elevation; a section between 2,300 and 4,900 feet in elevation; and the mountainous area, with elevations of over 4,900 feet. Wet, tropical forests make up a large part of the lowlands in the central Isthmus, where the Canal Zone is located.

Climate. Because of nearness to the equator, there is only slight seasonal variation in Panama.

The average annual temperature of the lowlands is approximately eighty degrees. Rain occurs year-around on the coastal areas, with the maximum—between 59 and 138 inches annually—falling on the Caribbean Coast. The Pacific Coast area receives between 59 and 79 inches of rainfall annually.

Capital City. Panama City.

Population. The total population of Panama, exclusive of the Canal Zone, is about 1.5 million; the population of Panama City (on the Pacific Ocean end of the Canal) is nearly 600,000; the population of Colon (on the Caribbean end of the Canal) is about 70,000; the population of the Canal Zone, just previous to the signing of the treaty that was to turn the Canal over to the Panamanians, was over 40,000, about 6,000 of whom were North Americans.

Ethnic Makeup. The ethnic cross-section of the entire Panamanian population is varied, with North Americans, Chinese, Negroes (from the Caribbean area), Spaniards, Italians, Greeks, and others.

Language. The official language of Panama is Spanish; however, many of the workers in the Canal Zone—and particularly in the Free Zone—also speak and understand English.

Currency. United States dollar and Panamanian coins.

Transportation. The Panamanian transportation system in the industrialized area is extensive and efficient. The Trans-Isthmian Highway joins Panama City with Colon. The National Highway connects Panama City to Costa Rica, and there is a highway to the Colombian border. A forty-nine-mile-long transisthmian railroad operates between Panama

City and Colon, and a railroad operates between La Concepcion and Puerto Armullas, on the Pacific Coast. A railway system serves the banana-growing area of Bocas del Toro. There are port facilities along both coastlines, with the best ports located at Cristobal, on one end of the Canal, and the Port of Balboa on the other end. There are international airports, as well as national airlines, that serve many Panamanian towns.

Communications. The national government owns and operates the communications systems, with the exception of two privately owned systems: Tropical Radio and Intercomsa. These systems provide telegraph, telephone, and radio communications.

Living Accommodations. There are multifamily dwelling rentals in the urban areas. Condominiums also provide living facilities.

Education. There are preelementary, elementary, secondary and university facilities in the Panamanian educational system. Among the several universities is the University of Panama. Literacy among the indigenous population is improving.

Medical. There are hospital, hospital clinics, health centers, mobile medical units, doctors, dentists and nurses available in Panama.

Recreation and Culture. Panamanian cultural institutions include the Panamanian Art Institute, the Concert Association of Panama, the National Conservatory, the School of Plastic Art, and the National School of Dance. The Panamanian Tourist Bureau works to preserve traditional holidays, folk music and the folk dances. The Panamanian Carnival is well known for its colorful costumes and beautiful music. The Institute of Culture and Sports promotes the Junior Olympiads and other interprovincial events.

Government. There were major changes in the Panamanian government in 1946, and again in 1968. In 1972, a constitutional form of government was established (critics of the Panamanian government still call it a dictatorship, however), and a 505-member assembly elected. On a local basis, the country is divided into nine provinces and a territory, with provinces divided into municipal districts, which are subdivided into counties. The head of each province is the governor, appointed by the president.

Political Stability. Political and social unrest in Panama is not unknown. Most of the unrest seems to manifest itself as riots, such as those experienced on U.S. campuses, rather than through any organized or concerted effort to change the government structure. Despite problems of the past, the tax haven business of Panama does not seem to have suffered.

Books to Read, Books to Avoid

Tax Havens for Corporations, Adam Starchild, 170 pages plus index, 1979. Gulf Publishing Company, Box 2608, Houston, Texas 77001.

I wrote it so I will not review it. Needless to say, I highly recommend it.

Mark Skousen's Complete Guide to Financial Privacy, Mark Skousen, 233 pages, 1979. Alexandria House, 901 N. Washington Street, Alexandria, Virginia 22314.

Most highly recommended. I wish I had written it. Any book that quotes me at length can't be bad.

How to Use Foreign Tax Havens, Marshall J. Langer, 383 pages, 1975. Practicing Law Institute, 810 Seventh Avenue, New York, New York, 10019.

Intended for lawyers only, a very good technical work. It is getting somewhat dated, but a new edition is expected. Definitely have your lawyer read it.

The Robert Kinsman Guide to Tax Havens, Robert Kinsman, 250 pages plus index, 1978. Dow Jones-Irwin, 1818 Ridge Road, Homewood, Illinois, 60430.

Written by a professional journalist rather than someone in the tax haven industry. I do not recommend it. Save your time and money.

Tax Havens of the World, Walter H. Diamond, two looseleaf volumes with update service. Matthew Bender, 235 E. 45th Street, New York, New York, 10017.

This is intended for lawyers, and is a guide to all tax haven countries. The price is about $100, and there are some glaring errors.

How To Do Business Tax Free, Midas Malone, 158 pages (of large type), 1976. Enterprise Publishing Company, 1300 Market Street, Wilmington, Delaware 19801.

Not at all recommended. It is simplistic and misleading.

Index

alienation, principle of, 34, 36
articles of incorporation and articles of association, 72–76, 114; in the Bahamas, 113–114; in Bermuda, 118–19; in the Cayman Islands, 126; in Hong Kong, 152–53; in Liberia, 158–60; in Liechtenstein, 208–11; in the New Hebrides, 132–33; in Panama, 143–44, 148

Bahamas, The, 107, 108–15, 120, 121, 122, 135, 155, 225–27; accessibility, 109, 226; banking and currency, 110–11, 226; climate, 108, 225; education, 226, 227; exports, 108–9; Freeport, 112; government, 109–10, 227; location, 108, 225; Nassau, 108, 226; New Providence, 108, 109, 112; population, 108, 226–27; tax laws, 111–12; topography, 225
Barbados, 52, 181–82, 227–28; Bridgetown, 227; economy, 228; government, 228; location, 181, 227; population, 228; taxes,

Bermuda, 37, 107, 115–20, 121, 122, 135, 136–37, 228–30; accessibility, 115–16, 229; banking and currency, 117, 229; "Bermudization," 120; climate, 229; education, 229; financial burdens of incorporation, 119; General Corporation Law, 118; government, 116, 120, 230; Hamilton, 229; location, 228; population, 229; professional services available, 117, 229; racial tensions, 120, 230; Registrar of Companies, 118; tax laws, 116, 117–18, 120; topography, 228
British Virgin Islands, 52, 101, 178–81, 230–32; accessibility, 178–79, 232; Anegada, 178; British-American Trust Co., 180; climate, 178, 231; compared with the Netherlands Antilles, 180, 181; currency, 179, 181–82; topography, 227
231; education, 232; government, 179, 232; Jost Van Dyke, 178; location, 230; population, 231; professional services available, 179; taxes, 178, 180–81; topography, 231; Tortola, 178, 231; Virgin Gorda, 178

Canadian provinces, 175
Carlos, Juan (king of Spain), 131
Cayman Islands, 107, 108, 121–28, 135, 146, 148, 154, 233–34; accessibility, 122, 233; banking and insurance regulations, 127–28, 233; Cayman Brace, 121; compared with Bermuda and the Bahamas, 121, 122, 123, 124, 127, 128; compared with the New Hebrides, 128, 133; corporate legislation, 123–25; court structure, 123; Georgetown, 233; government, 123, 234;

Grand Cayman, 121, 233; Little Cayman, 121; location, 233; population, 121, 123, 233; professional services available, 124, 126; Registrar of Companies, 124; significance of crown colony status, 123; taxes, 122; topography, 233
Chase Manhattan Bank, 28
civil law tradition (Code Napoléon), 82–83, 173, 183–84
common law tradition, 82–83, 106, 110, 115, 116, 123, 126, 132, 151, 153, 179
corporations, 35–36, 50–56, 65–79, 87, 161, 183; holding companies, 50–51, 59, 71, 153–54
Costa Rica, 152, 160–67, 233, 234–35; accessibility, 162, 235; climate, 162, Commercial Registry, 165, Costa Rican Export Promotion Law, 163; economy, 162, 234; education, 235; government, 162, 235; investment possibilities, 163–64, 165–66; Law 4812, 161–62, location, 234; population, 162, 234; professional services available, 235; taxes, 163; topography, 234; San José, 167, 234

Delaware laws of 1927, 143, 157
Diamond, Walter H. *(Tax Havens of the World)*, 248

Gramco, 48

Holland, 175
Hong Kong, 136, 148–54, 186, 217, 235–37; accessibility, 148–49, 150, 236, 237; climate, 236; and Communist China, 149; compared with Liechtenstein, 186; compared with Switzerland, 217; "Cuba clause," 154; currency, 150; educa-

251

tion, 237; government, 150–51, 236; holding companies, 153–54; location, 235; population, 149, 236; professional services available, 150, 236; taxes, 150, 151–52; topography, 235; Victoria, 236
Hungarian bank accounts, 30

incorporation. See corporations
Information Center, The, Overseas Private Investment Corporation, 163, 164
Internal Revenue Service (IRS), 13, 14–15, 16, 17, 22, 40, 41, 42, 49, 53–54, 56, 57, 70, 83, 88, 90–91, 92–93, 94–97, 100, 107, 171, 181, 183, 186, 192, 222; capital gains, 44, 79, 89–90; corporate income tax, 98; death tax, 58; dividends, 89, 90; double taxation agreements, 100–101, 107, 169–72, 173, 176–78, 180–81, 220–21; estate tax, 58, 79; multitier taxation arrangements, 107; personal income tax, 87–92; probate, 58, 79; Subpart F, 14–15, 40, 41, 44, 48, 50, 53, 55, 56, 58, 60, 61, 70, 91, 94, 96, 97, 171, 176, 186, 192
international trade: banks, 59–60; finance companies, 59–60; insurance companies, 60; manufacturing, 60; shipping, 61; technical, 62
IOS, 48
Israel, 31

Kinsman, Robert *(The Robert Kinsman Guide to Tax Havens),* 248

Langer, Marshall J. *(How to Use Foreign Tax Havens),* 247
Liberia, 61, 142, 154–60, 237–39; accessibility, 156, 238–39; background, 154–55;

climate, 238; corporate regulations, 157–59; currency, 156; exports and imports, 155; government, 155, 156, 239; location, 154, 155, 237; Monrovia, 156, 159, 238; population, 238; professional services available, 156; taxes, 156–57, topography, 238

Liechtenstein, 23, 30, 66, 83, 97, 183–215, 217, 239–40; accessibility, 184, 239–40; banking and currency, 185–86, 207, 239; climate, 239; code of civil law, 184–85; compared with Hong Kong, 186; establishments *(Anstalts)*, 200–207; foundations *(Stiftungs* or *Familienstiftungs)*, 186–200; government, 184, 200; location, 184, 239; population, 239; taxes, 185, 186, 207, 212–213, 215; topography, 239; Vaduz, 239

Malone, Midas *(How To Do Business Tax Free)*, 248

Minerva Consulting Group, Inc., 224

Netherlands Antilles, 52, 101, 172–78, 240–41; accessibility, 172; Aruba, 173; Bonaire, 173; climate, 172; compared with British Virgin Islands, 180, 181; Curacao, 172, 173; freeport, 178; government, 172–73, 241; location, 172, 240–41; population, 172; taxes, 175–78; Willemstad, 241; Windward Islands, 173

New Hebrides, The, 128–33, 135, 241–43; accessibility, 128–29, 242; climate, 242; compared with Cayman Islands, 133; currency, 132; economic activities, 129; education, 242; location, 241; Nagri Gramal, 130–31; political structure, 130–

31, 243; professional services available, 132, 243; social structure, 129–30, 242; taxes, 132; topography, 241; Vila, 242

offshore funds, 43–50, 59; in the Bahamas, 113

Panama, 61, 137–48, 154, 243–46; accessibility, 137–38, 139–40, 142, 244–45; banking and currency, 139, 142, 147, 148, 244; Canal Zone, 139; climate, 137, 243–44; Colon, 137; Colon Free Zone, 146–47, 148; corporate laws, 143, 145–46, 147; education, 245–46; government, 138–39, 246; Inter-American Highway, 138; location, 243; Panama Canal, 137; Panama City, 137, 244; population, 137, 244; professional services available, 140, 147, 245; shipping industry, 142, 148; taxes, 140–41, 142, 145, 147; topography, 243

Pan-American Airways, 238–39

Retirees Club of Costa Rica, 167
Rhodesia, 26, 30
Royal Dutch Shell, 93

Sharples, Sir Richard, 230
Skousen, Mark *(Mark Skousen's Complete Guide to Financial Privacy)*, 247
Starchild, Adam, *(Tax Havens for Corporations)*, 247
Surinam, 175
Switzerland, 175, 184, 185, 217–22; accessibility, 218; (Swiss) bank accounts, 30, 111, 139, 207, 217, 218, 221; currency, 215, 218, 219; corporate laws, 221; economy, 217–18; government, 217, 218; population, 218; professional services

available, 218; taxes, 219–21

tax avoidance and tax evasion, distinction between, 13–14, 17, 18–19, 54–56, 96–98
trusts, 50, 57–58, 59, 65, 79–85, 87, 161; in the Bahamas, 115; in Bermuda, 119–20; in the Cayman Islands, 126–27, 214; "Cuba clause," 115, 175; exchange controls, 173–74; in Hong Kong, 153–54, 214; in Liberia, 160; in Liechtenstein, 183–84, 186; 213; in Netherlands Antilles, 173; in The New Hebrides, 133

United States Congress, 84, 93, 155, 176
United States Constitution, 56, 155
United States Department of Justice, 222
United States Tax Code. *See* Internal Revenue Service
United States Virgin Islands, 178, 179